About Wa

GRAFFEG

Published by Graffeg
First published 2006
Copyright © Graffeg 2006
ISBN 0 9544334 7 5

Graffeg,
Radnor Court, 256 Cowbridge Road
East, Cardiff CF5 1GZ Wales UK.
Tel: +44(0)29 2037 7312
sales@graffeg.com www.graffeg.com
Graffeg are hereby identified as the
authors of this work in accordance
with section 77 of the Copyrights,
Designs and Patents Act 1988.

Distributed by the Welsh Books
Council www.cllc.org.uk
castellbrychan@cllc.org.uk

A CIP Catalogue record for this
book is available from the British
Library.

Designed and produced by
Peter Gill & Associates
sales@petergill.com
www.petergill.com

Map base information reproduced
by permission of Ordnance Survey
on behalf of HMSO
© Crown Copyright (2005).
All rights reserved. Ordnance
Survey Licence number 100020518

About Wales
Written by David Williams, foreword
by Siân Lloyd

The publishers are also grateful to
the Welsh Books Council for their
financial support and marketing
advice. www.gwales.com

Every effort has been made to
ensure that the information in this
book is current and it is given in
good faith at the time of publication.
Please be aware that circumstances
can change and be sure to check
details before making travel plans.

About
Wales

GRAFFEG

Foreword

"Whether you live here or are visiting for the first time, I hope that this book will inspire you to explore Wales's many cultural and historical treasures, leading you to new and exciting experiences. It is intended to be a source book of ideas for things to do."

Left:
Conwy Castle.
Conwy has the most complete circuit of medieval town walls in the UK, over a kilometre in circumference and guarded by twenty-one towers and three impressive double-towered gateways (more see page 37).

Wales is a remarkable part of the world, in which many centuries of human settlement and endeavour have created a rich and fascinating heritage. From battle-worn castles to settled market towns and villages, and from the tough working environments of mines and quarries to the elegance of the grandest historic houses, there are tremendous places to visit.

Museums across the land are able to draw upon wonderful original material to tell our story. Many towns have small museums specialising in local history. The National Museum Wales is a world-class group of museums and galleries where our collective past is illuminated by means of amazing original material, authoritative explanation and the latest display technology.

Our conspicuous enthusiasm for culture, especially music and literature, is famous around the world. Wales produces a remarkable number of international stars of concert hall, opera, stage, screen and rock arena – along with many gifted writers and poets. There is strength in depth, from keen amateur activity in local halls and eisteddfodau to the thriving professional creative sphere, which is a significant employer.

....

Our conspicuous enthusiasm for culture, especially music and literature, is famous around the world. Wales produces a remarkable number of international stars of concert hall, opera, stage, screen and rock arena – along with many gifted writers and poets.

....

There are major festivals, and year-round programmes of events, at which every cultural and artistic activity – music, literature, theatre, dance, the visual arts and others – may be enjoyed.

Wales confidently asserts its cultural individuality in an increasingly interconnected and globalised world. The long history of the Welsh people has evolved into a forward-looking modern identity, based on respect for the past.

As someone who lives in both England and Wales, and travels widely, I enjoy sharing this distinctive sense of knowing who I am with people I meet.

The Welsh language – spoken by around half a million people from a population of just under 3 million – is the everyday language of many communities. I am fluently bilingual in Welsh and English and applaud the decision of my parents, not Welsh speakers themselves, to send me to a Welsh school. The education I received there – including opportunities in public speaking, drama and music – set me on course towards becoming a broadcaster.

The language gives access to an amazing literature and supports a thriving culture. But it is not an exclusive indicator of Welshness, as the majority of the population will testify. English and Welsh enjoy official status together – in public life, business, the media and education – and many other languages are heard, especially in the multicultural seaport and university cities of Cardiff, Newport and Swansea.

Whether you live here or are visiting for the first time, I hope that this book will inspire you to explore Wales's many cultural and historical treasures, leading you to new and exciting experiences. It is intended to be a source book of ideas for things to do. So please enjoy the evocative photographs and learn interesting things but, above all, be sure to get out and about to experience these wonders of Wales for yourself!

Siân Lloyd

Introduction

This book celebrates the historical and cultural attractions that make Wales such a special place. We hope that it will lead you to enjoyable new discoveries and a deeper appreciation of this ancient and profoundly fascinating land and its people.

Located on the western side of the UK, it is bounded by the sea on three sides and shares a long land border with England to the east. Much of the natural environment is truly extraordinary – almost a quarter of the area of Wales enjoys special designation. There are three national parks – Snowdonia, the Brecon Beacons and the Pembrokeshire Coast – containing landcapes and habitats of international importance. Other regions – the coasts of Anglesey and the Llŷn peninsula, the Clwydian Hills, Gower and the Wye Valley – are Areas of Outstanding Natural Beauty. There are more than 1,000 Sites of Special Scientific Interest, including some of the most important wildlife areas in Europe.

But it is the way in which people have left their mark – on the landscape, in towns and cities, and on the world – that gives Wales its unique character. It is a place where a powerful sense of history, and the achievements of those who went before, are valued by an advanced modern nation.

It is the way in which people have left their mark – on the landscape, in towns and cities, and on the world – that gives Wales its unique character.

Along with England, Scotland and Northern Ireland, Wales is part of the United Kingdom. It is therefore not a nation state in the full sense – but its people certainly see themselves as a distinct nation, with a clear identity. The survival of the Welsh language reinforces this distinctiveness for many, but people who don't speak the language are also quick to point out that they are proud to be Welsh. The devolution of significant powers from Parliament in London to the National Assembly for Wales in Cardiff has given us one of the world's newest democratically elected institutions, having a declared intention to make its deliberations as open and accessible as possible.

Evidence of the ways in which people lived and worked over the centuries is preserved at our many ancient monuments, castles, historic houses and places of industry. The great medieval castles of north Wales and the industrial landscape of Blaenavon in the south-east are UNESCO World Heritage Sites. Many places are in the care of either the National Trust or Cadw, the Welsh Assembly Government's historic environment division, which looks after historic sites, buildings and monuments. Our museums and galleries, including the National Museum Wales, tell the story of our remarkable past.

The Welsh are, by justifiably deserved reputation, seen as a musically and lyrically gifted people. Ability in these areas is cherished and nurtured, and enjoyed at countless local events and numerous major festivals across the land. The eclectic diversity of cultural life reflects the cosmopolitan nature (especially in the cities) and open-minded instincts of the people – along with their typically gregarious disposition towards the more sociable aspects of life!

This book celebrates the historical and cultural attractions that make Wales such a special place. We hope that it will lead you to enjoyable new discoveries and a deeper appreciation of this ancient and profoundly fascinating land and its people.

David Williams

Castles

Heritage

Festivals

Events

About this book

About Wales gives you guidance on visiting cultural and heritage places and events with overviews on castles and heritage, museums and galleries, festivals and events. The four regional sections, north, mid, south west and south east, have a map showing locations, main roads and National Parks. Each area is packed with ideas on where to visit and what to do, with contact information and web addresses.

This book includes visitor information, Tourist Information Centre contact details, websites for more information, places to stay and eat, with an introduction on the Welsh language and how to find your way around Wales. There's also a fully indexed list of all the places, attractions, festivals and events at the back of the book.

We hope you will enjoy browsing in search of interesting places to visit and things to do.

Contents

Top left to right:
Pembroke Castle is a formidable fortress occupying an excellent defensive position overlooking the estuary.

Pentre Ifan surely commemorates someone of great importance during those distant times.

National Waterfront Museum has information technology of the entertaining and visitor-friendly variety.

National Museum Cardiff contains a superb collection of French Impressionist paintings.

Museums

Galleries

Where to stay

Where to eat

Below left to right:
Brecon Jazz Festival has a friendly atmosphere with concerts given by jazz legends.

Llanwrtyd Wells is where you are likely to encounter some pretty unusual goings-on.

Harbourmaster, Aberaeron has an imaginative menu based on fine local produce.

The Bear Hotel, Crickhowell is constructed in the style typical of a coaching inn.

Castles and heritage

Most of the many archaeological sites, castles and historic houses of Wales, and numerous former centres of industry, are in the care of one of two agencies – **Cadw** or the **National Trust**. It is said that if a historic property has a roof, then it is likely to be run by the National Trust; otherwise it is probably the responsibility of Cadw. Not an infallible guide, of course, but a helpful start.

Wales has more castles and fortifications for its area than anywhere else in Europe.

Wales has more castles and fortifications for its area than anywhere else in Europe. If you include every earthwork revealed by archaeological surveys and aerial photography, there are more than six hundred sites. Their number and variety reflect the nation's turbulent and fascinating history.

In prehistoric times, life was a constant struggle for survival against the elements and attack by others. The earliest inhabitants of Wales made stone tools and weapons, but their limited building abilities were mainly directed at ceremonial matters and the commemoration of their dead. Though primitive fortifications exist, they are not substantial.

The **Celtic tribes**, who lived throughout what we now call the UK and Ireland before the arrival of the **Romans**, were notoriously warlike. The landscape – especially coastal

Top left to right:
Chirk Castle,
Cardiff Castle,
Caerphilly Castle,
Gwydir Castle.

Below left to right:
Kidwelly Castle,
Conwy Castle,
Gwydir Castle,
Caernarfon Castle.

promontories and hilltops with good views – is peppered with the remains of their substantial forts.

The Romans introduced a sophisticated network of forts, barracks, roads and ports to sustain their legions as they encountered the troublesome tribes of the region they called **Cambria**. Many indigenous **Celts** eventually saw the advantage of adopting Roman ways, and their pragmatic co-operation made possible the governance of this remote extremity of the empire.

When the Romans began pulling out of their distant province of Britannia towards the end of the 4th century, the power vacuum was filled by regional rulers who provided the inspiration for the legendary **King Arthur**, mentioned for the first time in an early Welsh poem and later idealised into a paragon of chivalry.

The Saxons conquered much of what is now England but found Wales and Scotland fiercely resistant. During the 8th century, the eponymous **King Offa of Mercia**

ordered the building of his dyke, a low earthwork that marked the western limit of his ambition and recognised the separateness of Wales.

On the Welsh side of **Offa's Dyke**, regional kings and princes consolidated their rule. Their courts were usually peripatetic and their households – families, soldiers, servants, minstrels and poets – moved between several castles. Through war, treaty and marriage their territories began to coalesce into an emerging Welsh nation.

In 1039, **Gruffudd ap Llywelyn** became the first ruler of a united and independent Welsh nation that was organised upon a sophisticated legal and constitutional foundation. But this was not the best timing. Within a couple of decades of the arrival of **William the Conqueror** in 1066, the **Normans** had taken the lands and powers of the Welsh princes in much of south-eastern Wales and were extending their influence and building their solid castles throughout the lowlands.

In 1267, **Llywelyn ap Gruffudd** was recognised by **Henry III as Prince of Wales**, but this harmonious arrangement was also short-lived. The English king **Edward I**, who came to power in 1272, aimed to bring Wales and Scotland fully under his rule. He spent vast sums in building his 'iron ring' of castles around Gwynedd, from where Llywelyn mounted his campaigns to retain independence. Having succeeded in securing solid support throughout Wales against overwhelming forces, Llywelyn was eventually ambushed and killed at Cilmeri near Builth Wells in 1282.

Numerous fortified mansions and grand homes in the style of medieval castles have been built in Wales since those distant days of strife, but the pinnacle of castle building for military purposes was in the time of Edward I. The remarkable architecture and ingenuity of four of his castles – **Caernarfon, Conwy, Harlech and Beaumaris –** built by Master James of St George, the French genius in such matters, has been recognised in their

collective designation as a UNESCO World Heritage Site.

Until the mid-18th century, Wales was a largely rural nation where landowners enjoyed the resources to build fine houses, and agricultural workers and their families lived modestly. The coastline was dotted with small harbours where fishing was the main activity.

The largest structures were the castles, which had long since outlived their purpose, and the great religious buildings, including the ruins of medieval abbeys.

The Industrial Revolution rapidly transformed the working pattern, the economy, the built environment and the social fabric of Wales. Within a few decades, small towns and villages were transformed into some of the largest concentrations of industry in the world.

Merthyr Tydfil became the world's largest iron-producing centre, making possible the building of the railways. A pall of noxious fumes over **Swansea** and **Llanelli** reflected their specialisation in the

Top left to right: Menai Suspension Bridge, Tenby Tudor Merchant's House, Preseli Hills (memorial to poet Waldo Williams), Llanerchaeron.

Below left to right:
Caldey Abbey,
Bodnant Garden,
Plas Mawr,
Basingwerk Abbey.

smelting of copper, tin and other metals. Large numbers of people flocked to Wales from England and further afield, to provide manpower for the new industries.

The mining of coal in the south Wales Valleys boomed to the point where, by the early 20th century, 250,000 men toiled underground and **Cardiff** became the world's largest coal-exporting port. By this time, the combined population of the mining towns of the south Wales Valleys was equivalent – in number and variety of origin – to that of an additional large city.

The slate quarries of north and mid Wales expanded to meet the demand for roofing material at home, in Europe and in north America. Seaports grew to handle the thriving trade in raw materials and goods – and, as the railway network grew, to serve the passenger traffic to and from Ireland. Manufacturing industry expanded, particularly in south-eastern and north-eastern Wales.

Many of the industrial buildings and structures that made this ferment of activity possible – along with the grand houses built on its wealth – may be visited today. These heritage sites provide a fascinating insight into the way the people of Wales lived and worked in times gone by.

Several sites of the National Museum Wales (please see overleaf) provide especially direct insights into the industries that were so significant in shaping the appearance of the land and the character of the people.

The National Slate Museum, The National Wool Museum, The National Waterfront Museum, the St Fagans National History Museum and the Big Pit National Coal Museum combine informative displays with authentic buildings and machinery, and demonstrations of the skills involved. They are described at www.museumwales.ac.uk, where you will also find details of forthcoming exhibitions, talks, re-enactments and other events.

Museums and galleries

As befits a nation with such a rich history and well-preserved material heritage, Wales has many excellent museums.

The **National Museum Wales** is a widely dispersed group of leading institutions. The **National Slate Museum** in Llanberis, tells how the quarrymen extracted the versatile building and roofing material from the mountains, and describes their tough lives. The **National Wool Museum** in the Teifi valley is the place to try carding and spinning for yourself, and to learn all about wool production and use.

Few museums offer anything quite as dramatic as the underground tour at the **Big Pit National Coal Museum** near Blaenavon. And few put information technology to such effective use as the **National Waterfront Museum** in Swansea, which tells the story of the people of Wales at work, in industries old and new.

St Fagans National History Museum is one of Europe's very best open-air museums, featuring a wonderful collection of buildings relocated from all over Wales, together with absorbing indoor exhibitions about rural life and folk traditions.

The **Turner House Gallery** in Penarth is the smallest of the National Museums group, showing fine art of the highest quality. The **National Museum Cardiff** is the nation's storehouse of all that is best in many and varied fields of interest – from archaeology to zoology, decorative arts, fine art, geology, science, technology and many other areas.

In addition to the National Museums, you will find that most towns have a museum or heritage centre dedicated to the extraordinary variety of life and culture to be found in this deeply fascinating part of the world.

Top left to right: Oriel Mostyn Gallery, Museum of Modern Art, Bodelwyddan Castle, National Museum Cardiff.

Below left to right:
National Waterfront
Museum Swansea,
Theatr Mwldan,
National History
Museum, St Fagans,
National Museum
Cardiff.

Interesting museums include the **Llangollen Motor Museum** and **Pendine Museum of Speed,** the **National Coracle Centre,** which displays coracles from all over the world, the **Rhondda Heritage Park** and the **Blaenavon World Heritage Museum,** a testimony to the pre-eminence of south Wales as the world's major producer of iron and coal in the 19th century.

Wales has a long tradition of artistic expression, which continues today. Many gifted artists and craftspersons live and work here and their work is sold from galleries and studios across the land. Collections of fine art, from Wales and elsewhere, have been assembled both by the nation and by individual collectors.

National Museum Cardiff displays many treasures including a significant collection of Impressionist works by Renoir, Monet and Cézanne. Eminent Welsh artists also feature, including 18th century landscape pioneers Richard Wilson and Thomas Jones, and 20th century artists Augustus John, Gwen John and Ceri Richards.

The **National Portrait Gallery** in Wales has over 100 portraits from the 19th century collections including works by John Singer Sargent and the Pre-Raphaelites.

The westernmost regions of Wales (especially Anglesey, Snowdonia and Pembrokeshire) have inspired many artists. Look out for pleasing depictions of landscape, seascape, the seasons and rural life by Sir Kyffin Williams RA, William Selwyn, Rob Piercy, John Knapp-Fisher, Donald McIntyre and others.

Clusters of high-quality artists' studios may be found at Glynllifon (near Caernarfon), Ruthin, Hay-on-Wye and St Clears.

The biennial **Artes Mundi** competition at the **National Museum Cardiff** features the work of international conceptual artists.

Festivals and events

There are festivals in Wales for just about every aspect of culture. You will find everything from large national events to local musical and literary festivals, carnivals, regattas and shows that draw the crowds to historic villages, towns and harbours.

You will find everything from large national events to local musical and literary festivals, carnivals, regattas and shows that draw the crowds to historic villages, towns and harbours.

The main tourism season in Wales extends from Easter onwards, through the summer, until the school term begins in early September. Countless events, suitable for all the family, are organised during these months. Many places also provide ample reason to visit throughout the year, by organising activities and entertainment appropriate to autumn, Christmas, and other times.

Musical, literary and theatrical enthusiasms feature strongly and you will find performances at every level from professional venue to village hall. The orchestra of **Welsh National Opera** and the **BBC National Orchestra of Wales** appear at spectacular open-air concerts each summer; at Swansea's Proms in the Park, Cardiff Bay and elsewhere.

Musical styles ranging from classical to brass bands, and from jazz to folk and

Top left to right: Aberystwyth and Ceredigion County Show, National Eisteddfod, Welsh National Opera concert at Cardiff Bay, The Big Cheese, Caerphilly.

Below left to right:
Abergavenny Food
Festival, Royal
Welsh Agricultural
Show, Builth Wells,
Blaenavon
Ironworks,
Cardigan Bay
Seafood Festival.

roots music, have strong followings at festivals, halls and clubs across the land. Authentic Welsh folk traditions, including music and dance, are still celebrated, notably in and around Cardiff, at the beginning of May and at Christmas and New Year.

The traditions of the countryside are a recurrent theme, central to the identity of many Welsh people. Despite the demands of the farming life, the seasonal pattern allows time for the agricultural shows at local and national level. The largest of these, the **Royal Welsh Agricultural Show** is held at Builth Wells during **July**, with the **Winter Fair** following at the same venue early in **December**. Smaller shows, to which all are welcome, are organised at county level throughout Wales.

Some of the more vigorous, and occasionally dangerous, traditional sports have disappeared but Wales has made a unique contribution in this area of endeavour. The little town of **Llanwrtyd Wells** has become famous for its calendar of what can only be described as profoundly wacky challenges, including the **world bog-snorkelling championships**! The latter requires an unusual ability to ignore the cold and unsavoury surroundings, and to navigate in zero visibility, as you swim as rapidly as you can for the finish line.

Llanwrtyd Wells has become famous for its world bog- snorkelling championships!

The largest annual events arrive one after the other during the spring, summer and early autumn. Typically organised by experienced professionals supported by resourceful local committees, they feature big names in their respective fields and provide a visitor experience second-to-none.

The Hay Festival of Literature, held each May, sees world-famous authors, and enthusiastic readers .

The **Hay Festival of Literature**, held each **May**, sees world-famous authors, and enthusiastic readers who appreciate a good book, congregating at the small town of Hay-on-Wye, which has more than 30 bookshops.

Brecon pulsates to the sounds of jazz during **August**, when traditional bands and skilled solo practitioners of the more rarified forms come to town for the **Brecon Jazz Festival**.

Bryn Terfel, the world's leading bass-baritone, invites world-class guests to join him on stage before an enthusiastic home audience at his annual **Faenol Festival** (voted Best Show in Wales) held near Bangor each **Augus**t Bank Holiday.

The **Cardiff Festival** offers an exciting series of concerts, a multicultural carnival, a harbour festival, food shows, sports competitions and many other events throughout the summer, in the city centre and at Cardiff Bay.

The Cardiff Festival offers an exciting series of concerts throughout the summer.

Celebrations of food and produce, including the **Abergavenny Food Festival**, make a point of inviting local companies to provide the best possible food and drink – both home-produced and more exotic.

The largest of Wales's cultural festivals – in fact, one of the largest in Europe, with a daily attendance typically exceeding 20,000 – is the **National Eisteddfod**. This week-long gathering follows a tradition established by Lord Rhys at Cardigan Castle in 1176, whereby poets and musicians (and nowadays many other

Top left to right: Bryn Terfel's Faenol Festival, Snowdonia, National Eisteddfod, Abergavenny Food Festival, Brecon Jazz.

Below left to right:
Hay-on-Wye literary
Festival,
Llandrindod Wells
Victorian Festival,
Cardiff Festival.

talented and creative participants) meet in a spirit of friendly competition.

The largest of Wales's cultural festivals – in fact, one of the largest in Europe, with a daily attendance typically exceeding 20,000 – is the National Eisteddfod.

Held at the beginning of **August**, the **National Eisteddfod** moves to a different part of Wales each year. The enormous pavilion, venue for competitions and evening concerts, seats some 3,500 people. The surrounding Maes, or campus, has several smaller performance and exhibition spaces and upwards of 300 stands, where most of Wales's cultural and educational organisations are represented.

The central point of the **National Eisteddfod** is that everything happens in the Welsh language. Simultaneous-translation receivers are available at the main entrance and anyone wishing to learn the language will be made welcome at the Learners' Pavilion – there's a hotly contested prize for Welsh Learner of the Year.

The principle of friendly competition has been extended worldwide by the **Llangollen International Musical Eisteddfod**. This captivating multicultural gathering originated in 1947 as a means of bringing together like-minded people from all over war-ravaged Europe, one of its most moving moments being the first appearance by a choir from Germany in 1949. Performers of appropriately high ability nowadays travel from all over the world to attend in a spirit of shared appreciation. Little wonder then, that this is the only festival in the world to have been nominated for the Nobel Peace Prize.

North Wales

Dublin
Dun Laoghaire
Cemaes ● ● **Amlwch**
A5025
Holyhead ● Din Lligwy ● ● Moelfre
South Stack ● Llanddeusant ● ● Llanerchymedd
Trearddur Bay B5111 Penmon
B5109 Pentraeth **Llandudno** ● Great Ormes Head ● **Prestatyn**
Rhosneigr A5 **Llangefni** B5109 ● ● Rhos-on-Sea **Rhyl**
A4080 Llanfair PG ● Beaumaris ● **Conwy** ● Colwyn Bay ● **Rhuddlan**
Newborough **Menai Bridge** ● **Bangor** ● Llandudno ● Abergele
Britannia Bridge A55 Junction Bodelwyddan
Tal-y-cafn ● **St. Asaph**
Caernarfon B5106 A470 ● Llangernyw
Llanberis Trefriw ● **Denbigh**
A4086 A5 ● Llanrwst A5
Caernarfon Bay A487 A4085 Capel Curig ● Nebo
Llandwrog Dolwyddelan ● ● Betws-y-coed
A499 **Beddgelert** A498 B4406 ● Pentrefoelas
A498 **Blaenau Ffestiniog** A5
Nefyn B4417 Tremadog A487 W
A497 Criccieth **Porthmadog** A470 ● Corwen
Pwllheli Portmeirion Bala ● ● Llandrillo
Harlech Snowdonia National Park B4401
Y Rhiw ● Abersoch A494
Aberdaron
Bardsey Island
Cardigan Bay ● Dolgellau
● Corris
Castell-y-Bere A458
B4405 A470
● Machynlleth
A470

Irish Sea

Scale
Kilometres
0 2 4 6 8 10
0 1 2 3 4 5 6
Miles

Key
- - - - National Parks

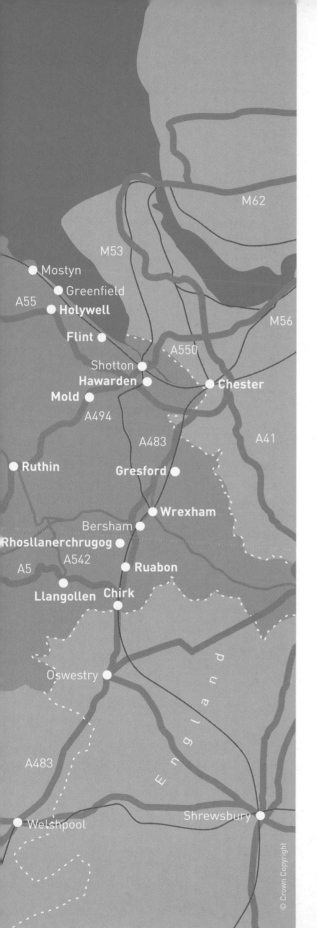

Welcome to north Wales, an enchanting area of striking contrasts. The Snowdonia National Park contains the highest mountains in England and Wales. The Llŷn peninsula, the Cambrian Coast and the Isle of Anglesey are places of fascinating history and heritage. The coastal resorts of Llandudno, Colwyn Bay, Rhyl and Prestatyn include everything that is exciting about the traditional seaside. The Borderlands have pretty country villages and an impressive array of castles and historic houses to explore.

Anglesey

Beaumaris Castle, Plas Newydd, Bryn Celli Ddu, Parys Mountain and delightful Moelfre. Cultural highlights include Oriel Ynys Môn, Beaumaris Festival, Ucheldre Centre and the Museum of Childhood.

Above:
Beaumaris Castle. The well preserved structure of Beaumaris Castle makes an impressive sight on the shore of the Menai Strait, with the mountains of Snowdonia beyond.

Amlwch

Amlwch Port. This intriguing harbour, a narrow, north-facing cove protected by breakwaters, was built in the late 18th century for the purpose of exporting copper from Parys Mountain. A thriving ship-building industry developed alongside this trade, reaching its peak in the late 19th century with the construction of a series of graceful schooners. The museum overlooking the harbour tells the story.
• From Amlwch, in north-eastern Anglesey, signs guide you to this remarkable place redolent of the past.
www.amlwchweb.com

Parys Mountain During the Bronze Age copper was extracted and put to use in this north-eastern corner of Anglesey, and the Romans also mined it here. But it was the Industrial Revolution that spurred new prospecting and brought the demand that made Parys Mountain the largest copper mine in Europe. A trail around the vast open cast scar gives amazing vistas of deeply coloured red, purple and yellow ores, but be sure to stay on the path, away from the deep and dangerous mine excavations.
• Inland from Amlwch, between the A5025 and the B5111.
Phone: 01407 832255
www.angleseyheritage.org

Moelfre – Royal Charter wreck.
A remarkable statue of Coxswain Richard Evans MBE, recipient of two RNLI gold medals for bravery, looks out over the bay from the Seawatch Centre, Moelfre. This coastline has seen many shipwrecks, including that of the sailing vessel Royal Charter, which was driven onto the rocks by a mighty storm in October 1859 within forty miles of her destination, Liverpool, at the end of a voyage from Australia. There were only forty survivors from some 490 passengers and crew. Charles Dickens visited the scene of the tragedy, which he

described in 'The Uncommercial Traveller'.
• An excellent footpath, which is surfaced for wheelchairs, leads from the village past the Seawatch Centre and the lifeboat station (often open in summer) to the site of the wreck.
Phone: 01248 410277

Beaumaris

The name of this attractive coastal town derives from the Norman "beau mareys", meaning beautiful marsh. From the pier and beach, which offer spectacular views of **Snowdonia**, to the castle and the character-filled streets with their wonderful mix of medieval, Georgian, Victorian and Edwardian architecture, this is an enchanting place to explore on foot.
• Some six miles from the A55 expressway as it crosses into Anglesey along the Britannia Bridge: follow the scenic and winding A545.
www.angleseyheritage.org

Beaumaris Castle. This is the last castle built for Edward I during his campaign to subjugate the people of Gwynedd. Along with his fortresses at Caernarfon, Conwy and Harlech, it enjoys UNESCO **World Heritage Site** status. Construction began in 1295, but the money ran out and the work was never finished. It is nevertheless an outstanding example of "walls within walls" construction, generally agreed to be the most perfectly realised castle in the UK. An attacker would have to breach four lines of fortification and fourteen separate defensive obstacles, beginning with a moat, while arrows rained down from ingeniously positioned slits.
• At the end of the main street in Beaumaris. There is parking nearby on The Green, the open area of grass between the town and the Menai Strait.
Phone: 01248 810361
www.cadw.wales.gov.uk

Beaumaris Gaol and Courthouse.
These atmospheric buildings give an insight into the harsh justice of times gone by. The courthouse, built in 1614, bears an entertaining mural showing two farmers in dispute over the ownership of a cow: one pulls at its horns, the other at its tail, while a lawyer milks away below. The Victorian gaol, with its gallows high on the walls, has the only working human treadmill in the UK.
• The historic buildings and attractions of Beaumaris are clearly signed and are within walking distance of the castle.
Phone: 01248 810921 (Gaol)
Phone: 01248 811691 (Court)
www.angleseyheritage.org

Museum of Childhood Memories, Beaumaris. In nine variously themed rooms at No.1 Castle Street – one of the impressive Georgian houses that characterise Beaumaris – you will find a treasure trove of memorabilia, toys and household items relating to the happier aspects of family life over the past 150 years. The displays will enthrall children, while bringing back many memories for the older generation.
• At the same end of Castle Street as the castle, close to the parking space on The Green.
Phone: 01248 712498
www.aboutbritain.com

Menai Suspension Bridge. The graceful span of Thomas Telford's suspension bridge, the first of its type in the world on such a scale, has been a familiar and attractive presence amid the scenic splendour of the Menai Strait since 1826. On the 30th of January of that year, the crowds cheered as the Royal London and Holyhead Mail Coach crossed over to Anglesey with its important cargo of mail bags bound for Dublin. It is possible to walk across the bridge – its construction is fascinating and the views are tremendous, while the tide flows at a remarkable rate through the arches.

Right:
Menai Strait.
Set against the backdrop of northern Snowdonia, Thomas Telford's suspension bridge across the Menai Strait occupies its place in the landscape with great dignity.

Above and far left:
Plas Newydd.
The attractions of Plas Newydd include the fine interiors, the woodland walk that takes you around the gardens, and the exciting programme of activities for all the family.

Left:
Britannia Bridge.
Massive steel arches have replaced the original tubular structure of the Britannia Bridge, which now carries both trains and cars over the Menai Strait.

• Narrow lanes lead down from the Anglesey end of the bridge to the small beach and quayside beneath.
www.angleseyheritage.org

Britannia Bridge. Robert Stephenson, son of the famous railway engineer George Stephenson, adopted an unusual design for his rail bridge, which was completed in 1850. To achieve the stiffness necessary to maintain the straightness of the rails under the weight of a train, while avoiding the use of an arch and the attendant loss of headroom for the masts of sailing ships passing below, he built a rectangular iron tube, similar in essence to a ship's hull. This served well until 1970, when it was accidentally set on fire. The present structure, supported by massive arches, has both rail and road decks.
• The bridges make a fine sight, set in the panorama of the Menai Strait and Snowdonia, from the top of the Marquess of Anglesey's column at Llanfair PG.
www.angleseyheritage.org

Plas Newydd. This elegant 18th century house, designed by James Wyatt and now in the care of the National Trust, is the ancestral home of the Marquess of Anglesey. It contains a magnificent 18m wide mural by **Rex Whistler** and other fine examples of his work. A military museum tells the story of the first Marquess who, having lost a leg while commanding the cavalry at the battle of Waterloo, was fitted with the first artificial leg to have sprung joints – and yes, this innovative device is on display.
• A couple of miles south-west of J8 on the A55 (for Llanfair PG), along the A4080. Phone: 01248 714795
www.nationaltrust.org.uk

Open-air theatre at Plas Newydd. The elegance of the impressive house is just one of the attractions of Plas Newydd. The surrounding woodland and fine gardens are a pleasure to behold in any season. Summer offers the additional delights of open-air performances of music and drama, including productions of Shakespeare.

Bryn Celli Ddu and Barclodiad y Gawres.
Anglesey, with its gentle landscape, fertile soil, mild maritime climate and convenient location at the centre of Irish Sea trade routes, has been populated since prehistoric times. The island has many important Neolithic monuments, including standing stones and burial chambers.
Barclodiad y Gawres is a passage grave containing stones inscribed with the spiral and zigzag designs also found elsewhere in Wales and in Ireland. **Bryn Celli Ddu** is a burial chamber overlying a "henge" used for religious ceremonies.
• Barclodiad y Gawres is south of Rhosneigr, on the A4080; Bryn Celli Ddu is off a minor road between the A4080, near Plas Newydd, and the village of Llanddaniel Fab.
www.cadw.wales.gov.uk

Oriel Ynys Môn. Anglesey's main heritage centre and art gallery is conveniently located just outside Llangefni. A permanent exhibition introduces the island's rich culture and history. An imaginative programme of temporary exhibitions and events encompassing art, craft, sculpture, music and social history provides plenty of reasons to visit throughout the year.
There is a café and a shop that sells local-interest books and the work of local artists, craft workers and jewellers.
• Just north of Llangefni, on the B5111 towards Llanerchymedd.
Phone: 01248 724444
www.angleseyheritage.org

Llys Rhosyr, Newborough. The independent Kingdom of Gwynedd, which emerged after the departure of the Romans and lasted until the death of Prince Llywelyn at the hands of Edward I's troops in 1282, had its power base in Anglesey. Its rulers divided their time between their courts at Aberffraw and Llys Rhosyr and their castles in Snowdonia. These foundations convey a potent sense of the loss that must have been felt as power was seized by Edward I, whose mighty castle at Caernarfon is in sight across the Menai Strait.
• Just outside the village of Newborough in southern Anglesey, along the minor road leading to Llanddwyn, near the church.
www.angleseyheritage.org

Llanfairpwllgwyngyllgogerychwyrndrobwllllantysiliogogogoch. Following the arrival of the railway during the 1850s, the enterprising villagers of Llanfair Pwllgwyngyll (as it was then known) sought ways of attracting trains and early tourists. In what would today be described as a stroke of marketing genius, a cobbler from Menai Bridge invented the longest name of any village anywhere, bringing the worldwide fame that continues to this day. The name, proudly displayed on the station and village shops (and on a gift shop in Cardiff, opposite the castle), means 'Saint Mary's Church in the hollow of the white hazel near a rapid whirlpool and the church of Saint Tysilio of the red cave'.
• Leave the A55 expressway just after it crosses the Britannia Bridge onto Anglesey and follow the A5 to the village.

Holyhead

Roman fort at Holyhead. Here, late in their history and at the far western limit of their conquests, the Romans, under increasing pressure to recall troops to defend the heart of their declining empire, built a small fort and naval base to guard against raiders from across the Irish Sea. It is said that Maelgwyn, the 6th century king of Gwynedd, gave the land within the walls of the fort to St Cybi as the site for a monastery, of which the present St Cybi's church is the successor.
• In the town centre. Seek out the outstanding stained glass windows by William Morris and the pre-Raphaelites.
www.holyhead.com

Left:
Llynnon Mill. The spinning sails of Llynnon Mill drive heavy millstones to grind flour in the traditional way, as windmills once did all over Wales.

Ucheldre Centre, Holyhead. Quality is the watchword at this powerhouse for the performing, literary and visual arts. Music and drama are staged in the beautiful and acoustically excellent chapel of the former Bon Sauveur convent. The adjoining exhibition gallery has an ever-changing programme of painting, sculpture and crafts, often supported by talks and classes. The licensed Ucheldre Kitchen prepares traditional recipes and the centre's shop has a good selection of books, music and gifts.
• Just outside the town centre, at Millbank, signed from the minor road past the park towards South Stack.
Phone: 01407 763361
www.ucheldre.org

Holyhead Maritime Museum. The seafaring traditions of the port of Holyhead are celebrated at this excellent maritime museum, run by knowledgeable volunteers and housed in the oldest lifeboat station in Wales, which dates from 1847. Displays of models, paintings, photographs and artefacts trace the town's history from Roman times to its present position as the UK's main ferry port for passenger and cargo services to Ireland.
• On Newry Beach, overlooking the large Outer Harbour, with views towards the breakwater and the ferries.
Phone: 01407 769745
www.angleseyheritage.org

· ·

Llynnon Mill. Anglesey's rich arable farmland has for many centuries produced an abundance of produce, both for local use and for sale further afield. Farmers brought wheat, barley, oats and other grains to one of the island's many windmills or watermills to be made into flour or animal feed. Llynnon is the only working windmill in Wales. The miller makes stoneground flour from organic wheat. He will be happy to explain the process and sell you a bag.
• Near Llanddeusant, signed from the A5025 and minor roads around Llanfaethlu.

Phone: 01407 730797
www.goanglesey.com

Swtan restored cottage. In its idyllic location at Church Bay on the west coast of Anglesey, the last traditional thatched cottage on Anglesey has been restored, and opens to the public each summer. With its cosy crogloft, where children would sleep, and large open hearth, it is typical of a style once common throughout rural Wales. Household and farm implements, and the well-tended vegetable garden give an insight into the labour intensive life of its former occupants.
• Between Llanfaethlu and Llanrhuddlad, north-east of Holyhead on the A5025: follow narrow lanes to Church Bay.
www.angleseyheritage.org

Iron Age settlements – Din Lligwy and Tŷ Mawr. The circular remains of ten stone huts at Tŷ Mawr, near Holyhead, once had conical roofs supported by wooden posts and thatched with straw or reeds. The site was occupied intermittently over a very long period, from Mesolithic times until the 6th century. The much grander compound of houses and working buildings at Din Lligwy, on the eastern side of Anglesey, evolved during the Roman occupation as the local Celtic chieftain adapted to the new ways.
• Tŷ Mawr is off the minor road from Holyhead to South Stack; Din Lligwy is signed from the A5025 and minor roads near Moelfre and Llanallgo.

· ·

Penmon

A remarkable cluster of buildings and monuments surrounds the holy well of St Seiriol, who lived at Penmon during the 6th century. The church dates from the 12th century. It houses two early Celtic crosses and has impressive Romanesque decoration. The associated Augustinian priory buildings were added a century later, and the nearby fishpond and dovecote are evidence of the self-sufficient lifestyle of the monks.

• A pleasant drive beyond Beaumaris, along the B5109.
www.angleseyheritage.org

South Stack

South Stack and Ellin's Tower. The spectacularly located lighthouse at South Stack was built in 1809 for the benefit of shipping navigating the busy Irish Sea. Buy a ticket at the **South Stack Café** for access to the island and a guided tour of the historic structure. The strenuous walk down, and then back up, some four hundred steps, giving magnificent close up views of seabird nesting sites, is most worthwhile. **Ellin's Tower** was built in 1868 as a summer house for the Stanley family, and named after their daughter; it is now an interpretive centre run by the Royal Society for the Protection of Birds.
• South Stack is a short drive, or a bracing walk around the mountain, from Holyhead. Ellin's Tower is off the approach road, near the café.
www.angleseyheritage.org

Festivals and events

Amlwch Viking Festival. Every two years, around the **end of July**, Amlwch commemorates the presence of the Vikings on Anglesey. Be ready to encounter authentically dressed warriors and villagers as they re-create the rivalry on the island after Viking raids, and re-enact the battle to expel the invaders.
Walk around a replica 10th century encampment, experience a Viking wedding and see craftsmen at work. Join the throngs of people at Amlwch Port to witness the ceremonial boat burning and fireworks display.
• Park away from the narrow quaysides of Amlwch Port. There are good vantage points on footpaths above the harbour.
www.amlwchvikingfestival.co.uk

Anglesey County Show. The Anglesey County Show is held annually in **August**. It is a large event organised for the buying and selling of animals, farm vehicles,

Above left:
Moelfre. Sculpture of seafaring hero Coxswain Richard Evans MBE.

Above:
Celtic cross. This fine Celtic Cross commemorates Anglesey's 18th century intelltuals, the Morris brothers.

Above right:
South Stack. An incomparable place for exhilarating clifftop walks.

Right:
Amlwch Port. Built in the late 18th century.

agricultural services and equipment. But earning a living from the land has been central to the identity and character of many of the island's inhabitants for centuries. The main ring and exhibition stands showcase both traditional skills and modern methods, and the show is a great place to experience the camaraderie typical of the farming community.
• Held at the County Showground near Mona, well signed from the A55.
Phone: 01407 720072
www.anglesey-show.freeserve.co.uk

Anglesey Oyster and Welsh Food Fair. Early October sees the food cognoscenti heading towards Trearddur Bay for the Anglesey Oyster and Welsh Produce Festival. There they will find a wide selection of Welsh food producers, along with a full programme of demonstrations and competitions. **Halen Môn** (Anglesey Sea Salt), **Gorau Glas** blue cheese and the varied delights of the **Deri Fawr smokery** are but a few examples of the wealth of fine produce grown or produced locally.
• The village and attractive beaches of Trearddur Bay are a couple of miles to the south of Holyhead, on the B4545.
www.angleseyoysterfestival.com

Beaumaris Festival. The Beaumaris Festival was founded in 1986 and has grown into a popular and prestigious event attracting international performers of the highest calibre. Held over the **May** Bank Holiday weekend, and a few days either side, it provides a feast of classical music, jazz, talks, theatre, poetry and art. The festival also features recitals by young performers, giving audiences a chance to hear a range of talented singers and instrumentalists before they become famous.
• Programme from local hotels and libraries.
Phone: 01248 714678
www.beaumarisfestival.co.uk

Cemaes Celtic Festival. The biennial Cemaes Celtic Festival hosts artists from the other Celtic nations – Ireland, Scotland, the Isle of Man, Cornwall and Brittany – as well as Wales, over the **August** holiday weekend. Run entirely by community volunteers, and supported by local businesses, it provides an important boost to the economy of this attractive harbour village, as well as being an entertaining day out.
• Cemaes is on the north coast of Anglesey, on the A5025.

Holyhead Maritime Festival. A lively programme of maritime events, both afloat and ashore, including regattas and air-sea rescue displays, brings the crowds to Holyhead's outer harbour each **August.** There are great viewing positions along the promenade at Newry Beach. This is one of the best harbours in the whole of the Irish Sea. Breakwater Park is the place to learn about the construction of the amazing sea wall.
• There is parking along the upper road along Newry Beach and towards the Coastguard Station, or you can walk the modest distance from the town centre.

Island Arts Week. Established by the Anglesey Arts Forum to celebrate the wealth of creative talent to be found on the island, Island Arts Week held each **April** includes workshops, talks, exhibitions, music and dance at venues all over Anglesey. Painters and sculptors open their studios, so that people may see the artists at work, and a wide range of high-quality items is available to buy at the craft fair.
• Details from local art and craft galleries and studios.
Phone: 01407 763361
www.angleseyartsforum.org

Llandudno, Colwyn Bay, Rhyl and Prestatyn

Great Orme, Llandudno Victorian Trail, Bryn Euryn Iron Age fort, the Alice in Wonderland Centre, the Punch and Judy show, Venue Cymru, Oriel Mostyn Gallery, Theatr Colwyn and Rhyl Pavilion.

Above and right: **Conwy Castle.** Walk around the town walls and you will see that Conwy still has its medieval layout of narrow streets from the quayside to the castle.

Colwyn Bay

Theatr Colwyn. This theatre features a vibrant programme of drama, music, dance and pantomime. The 386-seat auditorium also operates as a cinema.
• Colwyn Bay is served by J21 and J22 on the A55 expressway.
Phone: 01492 534263
www.theatrecolwyn.co.uk

Conwy

Conwy Castle. This formidable fortress occupies an excellent defensive position on a rock overlooking the harbour, from which it could be supplied in time of siege. Conwy has the most complete circuit of medieval town walls in the UK, over a kilometre in circumference and guarded by twenty-one towers and three impressive double-towered gateways. Walk around the walls, and climb the castle's towers for magnificent views of the harbour in one direction and the mountains of Snowdonia in the other.

• Leave the A55 at J17 or J18. There's a car park next to the castle.
Phone: 01492 592358
www.cadw.wales.gov.uk

Conwy Visitor Centre. Discover the past and present of this fascinating town, through exhibitions and films at the Conwy Visitor Centre, in the shadow of the castle. Combine history and fun at the **Brass Rubbing Centre**, and take away an impressive memento.
• A short walk from the castle, towards the town square and High Street.
Phone: 01492 596288

The Smallest House in Britain. Originally built as a fisherman's cottage, this tiny house is squeezed between larger buildings on Conwy's quayside. Amazingly, its last occupant was six foot three inches (1.9m) tall even though the house only measures nine feet (2.9m) by five feet (1.5m).
• Parking on the quayside, reached via very narrow arches in the town walls, is limited.

Left:
Thomas Telford's bridge. Although built over 500 years apart, Conwy Castle and Thomas Telford's bridge over the estuary make a harmonious pairing.

Above:
Plas Mawr. The exterior of Plas Mawr exerts an impressive presence in the town centre – the ornate interiors are magnificently decorated in bright colours.

Royal Cambrian Academy. A treat for art enthusiasts and holidaymakers alike, this fine art gallery puts on a varied programme of exhibitions, including ones that tour, throughout the year. The visual delights range from works by academy members, who include some of the most distinguished artists currently working in Wales, to masterpieces by famous painters from the past.
• Just off Conwy's High Street, behind the Elizabethan house Plas Mawr.
Phone: 01492 593413
www.rcaconwy.org

Plas Mawr. At the heart of Conwy's medieval town centre, you will find the finest town house of the Elizabethan era in the UK. The Great Hall was built between 1576 and 1585 for the Welsh merchant Robert Wynn. It has many original furnishings and the decorative plasterwork has been restored to its original splendour. An audio tour describes the restoration of this architectural gem.

• Halfway down the High Street from the town square towards the quayside.
Phone: 01492 580167
www.cadw.wales.gov.uk

Aberconwy House. Dating from the 14th century, this timber-framed merchant's house has survived for more than six centuries. The furnished rooms, described in an audio-visual presentation, show daily life from different periods in its history. Ask about the musical events that are held here from time to time.
• In Castle Street.
Phone: 01492 592246
www.nationaltrust.org.uk

Conwy suspension bridge. The elegant suspension bridge between the present road and rail bridges across the river Conwy was designed and built by Thomas Telford and was completed in 1826. It is a pleasant walk across the bridge from the castle.
• Access to the bridge is via the tollhouse

at the distant end from the castle.
Phone: 01492 573282
www.nationaltrust.org.uk

Great Ormes Head

The Marine Drive around Great Orme is a masterpiece of Victorian road building, providing panoramic views to Anglesey and Snowdonia. From **Llandudno's promenade**, head past the pier to begin this thrilling five-mile (8km) one way route, as it clings to the cliffs before emerging at the West Shore. It is one of the UK's longest toll roads.
• You can also drive up to the summit of Great Orme from a junction part-way along the Marine Drive. Look out for stray sheep and feral goats.
Phone: 01492 575408
www.visitllandudno.org.uk

Great Orme tramway. Britain's only cable-hauled public tramway has been operating for more than a century and still uses the original Victorian carriages. The contrast with the cable cars passing high overhead could not be greater. A combined ticket enables you to go up to the summit on one and return on the other.
• The tramway begins at Victoria Station in Church Walk, near the upper end of the main shopping street. The cable cars go from Happy Valley near the pier.
Phone: 01492 879306
www.greatormetramway.co.uk

Great Orme Bronze Age copper mines. This is the oldest metal mine open to the public anywhere in the world. Copper ore was mined here 4,000 years ago during the early Bronze Age, and the site experienced a revival of activity in the eighteenth and nineteenth centuries. You may follow the ancient workings, the earliest of them excavated using bone and stone hand tools, to amazing caverns 150ft (45m) below ground.
• Part-way up the road to Great Ormes summit – parking is limited.
Phone: 01492 870447
www.greatormemines.info

Above:
The Great Orme tramway. Provides outstanding views over the wide sweep of Llandudno's North Shore promenade.

Above:
Llandudno. You don't need a boat to experience the sea air in Llandudno – a walk to the end of the marvellous pier will serve just as well.

Above right:
Great Orme. The limestone outcrop of Great Orme dominates Conwy Bay – visit the world's largest Bronze Age mines where copper ore was extracted 4,000 years ago.

Llandudno

Llandudno Pier and Promenade.
Traditional coastal attractions abound on and around Llandudno's impressive Victorian pier, built so that all could enjoy the views and the therapeutic sea air. There are amusement arcades, along with cafés and bars and a lively programme of entertainment in spring and summer.
• Going to the end of the pier, rather than admiring it from the promenade, really is worthwhile for views of the town and Great Orme.
Phone: 01492 876258
www.visitllandudno.org.uk

Llandudno Victorian Town Trail. Walking is a great way to explore the generally level town centre and promenade of Llandudno. The town's attractions include the **Victorian Town Trail** (leaflets available from Tourist Information Centres, the library and hotels), the **Home Front Experience,** which re-creates civilian life during the Second World War, and **Llandudno Museum.** Bus tours of the wider area as far as Conwy start from North Parade near the pier, and are accompanied by a trained guide.
• The fascinating town trail was created primarily for tourists between 1849 and 1912. There are fifteen viewing points marked by information boards.
www.visitllandudno.org.uk

Alice in Wonderland Centre, Llandudno.
The real Alice Liddell, who inspired Lewis Carroll to write his enchanting tales of Alice's Adventures in Wonderland, enjoyed summer holidays with her family at their house on Llandudno's West Shore. At this entertaining town centre attraction you may walk through the magical rabbit hole and into the stories yourself, and experience her adventures through colourful displays and recorded excerpts.
• Located in Trinity Square, off Mostyn Street, just east of the the centre of town.
Phone: 01492 860082
www.wonderland.co.uk

Left:
Llandudno Beach. The Blue Flag recognises the cleanliness of the beach, and its excellent facilities – there's usually something interesting happening too, from children's entertainment to lifeboat days and bandstand concerts.

Below:
Oriel Mostyn Gallery. Described as 'one of the most adventurous contemporary art venues in the country', Oriel Mostyn Gallery also features temporary exhibitions, educational workshops and events.

Llandudno Museum. Enjoy exploring the town's fascinating history, from spotting the footprint on a Roman tile, to visiting a traditional Welsh kitchen with its pots and pans, or to wondering at the many items that bring the town's role as a holiday resort to life. Temporary exhibitions show an ever-changing programme of items from the museum collections, and work by local artists.
• In Gloddaeth Street, with parking within walking distance.
Phone: 01492 876517
www.llandudno-tourism.co.uk/museum

Venue Cymru. This 1500-seat theatre, with its associated exhibition spaces and pleasant restaurant, has established itself as one of the leading live performance venues in Wales. Its diverse programme ranges from children's shows and pantomime to opera, Welsh music, ballet, rock and pop music, comedy and musical theatre. It also hosts exhibitions, political conferences and the popular **North Wales Country Music Festival.**
• On the promenade, with ample car parking nearby.
Phone: 01492 872000
www.venuecymru.co.uk

Oriel Mostyn Gallery. The Mostyn Art Gallery was established in 1901 by Lady Augusta Mostyn to show the work of the Gwynedd Ladies Art Society, making it the first gallery in the world built specifically for work by female artists. It is now one of the UK's premier contemporary, modern and fine art galleries and displays major exhibitions of Welsh and international art. The craft shop stocks handmade jewellery, ceramics and glassware ranging from the classic to the quirky, along with books, prints and cards.
• Next door to the main Post Office, 200 yards from Llandudno's railway station.
Phone: 01492 879201
www.mostyn.org

The Home Front Experience. Step back to the time of the Second World War and discover the dangers and difficulties that the civilian population faced then. The sights and sounds of air raids, rationing, digging for victory, make do and mend, and morale-boosting singalongs are evocatively re-created in displays and tableaux.
• In Llandudno's New Street, behind the church.
Phone: 01492 871032

Professor Codman's Punch and Judy Show. This is the real thing: an authentic performance of the raucous puppet show which, preserved and presented by several generations of the same family, has delighted audiences in Llandudno since the 1860s. The dysfunctional couple and their supporting cast of characters, including the crocodile and the policeman, are here waiting for you to cheer and boo!
• Follow the sounds of laughter amongst the gardens at the pier end of the promenade.
www.punchandjudy.com/codgal.htm

Llangernyw

Sir Henry Jones Museum, Llangernyw. This fascinating museum of rural life is the childhood home of Sir Henry Jones (1852-1922) who, from humble origins, went on to become an eminent Professor of Moral Philosophy at Glasgow University and an influential figure in education in Wales.
• The village of Llangernyw is on the A548, between J24 of the A55 and Llanrwst.
Phone: 01492 575571
www.sirhenryjones-museums.org

Rhos-on-Sea

Saint Trillo's chapel, Rhos-on-Sea. After the departure of the Romans, when what is now England fell to the Saxons, the Celtic saints who roamed Wales, Scotland and Ireland established their cells, monasteries and churches and kept the flame of Christianity alive. The church of Saint Trillo dates from the 6th century; its altar was

built directly over an existing holy well.
• Rhos-on-Sea – Llandrillo-yn-Rhos – is between Llandudno and Colwyn Bay, near J20 on the A55.
www.visitllandudno.org.uk

Harbour at Rhos-on-Sea. A plaque on an old section of stone wall, said to be the original quayside, claims that it was from here, in the year 1170, that Prince Madog ap Owain Gwynedd sailed westward and discovered America, 322 years before Columbus's voyage. Porthmadog also claims the honour of being his departure port. But strenuous attempts to prove the story, including research into apparent similarities between Welsh and the languages of certain Native American peoples, have proved inconclusive.
• The promenade here is a quiet alternative to the bustle of Llandudno.
www.visitllandudno.org.uk

Rhyl

Pavilion Theatre. With over a thousand seats, this is a large regional performance space, established in 1991 and designed to accommodate all types of theatre and music, together with exhibitions and conferences.
• Rhyl is reached by means of the A525 dual carriageway from J27 on the A55.
Phone: 0870 330 0000
www.rhylpavilion.co.uk

Tal-y-cafn

Bodnant Garden. As you explore its many delights, you will understand why this is described as one of the world's finest gardens. Formal Italianate terraces give tremendous views over the Conwy valley to Snowdonia. Spectacular woodland contains the UK's largest giant redwood and many other towering trees. The famous laburnum arch reaches its bright golden-yellow peak in May.
• Off the A470 some five miles south of Conwy.
Phone: 01492 650460
www.bodnant-garden.co.uk

Trefriw

Trefriw Woollen Mill and Spa. This working mill generates its own electricity from the rushing waters of the river Crafnant, as it descends to join the river Conwy. Traditional Welsh bedspreads and tweeds with their colourful geometric patterns have been produced here for a hundred and fifty years. At the nearby spa, learn about its establishment by the Romans and its popularity in Victorian times, and sample the spa water it still produces today.
• Trefriw is on the B5106 between Betws-y-Coed and Conwy, near Llanrwst.
Phone: 01492 640462
www.t-w-m.co.uk

Festivals and events

Llandudno Festival of Music and the Arts. During **July**, Llandudno's streets and entertainment venues offer a wealth of outdoor and indoor activity. There are lunchtime and evening concerts, organised walks, Welsh folk music and dancing, street entertainers, tea dances on the pier, poetry readings and much more.
• Programmes from libraries, the Venue Cymru Theatre box office and via the Arts Council of Wales website.
Phone: 01492 546506
www.north-wales-events.co.uk

Llandudno Victorian Extravaganza and Transport Festival. The orderly planning of Llandudno's attractive streets and promenade, which set the scene for the town's emergence as the most genteel of Victorian seaside resorts, was instigated in the 1840s by Lord Mostyn, the local landowner and Member of Parliament. The first weekend of **May** each year sees the return of the colourful costumes and traditions of those days. The **Transport Festival** attracts a large gathering of immaculately turned out classic and vintage vehicles.
• Programmes from Tourist Information Centre.
www.victorian-extravaganza.co.uk

North Wales Borderlands

Llangollen, St Winefride's Well, St Asaph Cathedral, Valle Crucis Abbey, the Pontcysyllte aqueduct, Erddig Hall, Llangollen International Musical Eisteddfod, Clwyd Theatr Cymru, Bodelwyddan Castle and Ruthin Craft Centre.

Above: **Bodelwyddan Castle.** At Bodelwyddan Castle in surroundings conducive to the enjoyment of great art, the National Portrait Gallery arranges a changing programme of exhibitions of its many treasures.

Bodelwyddan

Church of St Margaret, Bodelwyddan.

The remarkable 'Marble Church' of Bodelwyddan is one of the showiest of all Victorian showpiece churches. The founder of this lavish church was Margaret, daughter of Sir John Williams of Bodelwyddan Castle and widow of Henry Lord Willoughby de Broke. A wealthy and strong-minded woman, she was determined to commemorate her husband by building the finest possible church in the Gothic Revival style, an aim she more than achieved.

• An impressive sight from the A55 between J25 and J26, west of St Asaph.
Phone: 01745 584563
www.bodelwyddan-castle.co.uk

Bodelwyddan Castle – National Portrait Gallery.

Set in 260 acres of magnificent parkland, Bodelwyddan Castle is now an outstation of the National Portrait Gallery. The castle as seen today is a creation of Sir John Hay Williams, and dates from between 1830 and 1852, though the estate has medieval origins. Architects Hansom (he who designed the horse-drawn cab) and Welch were employed by Sir John to refurbish and extend the house, while further works at this time also resulted in a magnificent estate wall and formal garden.

• Between J25 and J26 on the A55 expressway.
Phone: 01745 584060
www.bodelwyddan-castle.co.uk

Chirk

Chirk Castle. Completed in 1310, Chirk's rather austere exterior contrasts with the elegant and comfortable staterooms inside, with their fine plasterwork, Adam-style furniture, tapestries and portraits. The castle, as you will see from a distance as you approach and pass through the ornate gates, is surrounded by extensive parkland and formal gardens. After four hundred years of continuous occupation, it is still

Far left:
Denbigh Castle. From its hilltop site, this atmospheric fortress offers magnificent all-round views of the Vale of Clwyd.

Left:
St Winefride's Well. The sacred and peaceful ambience of St Winefride's Well, after which Holywell is named, is reminiscent of Lourdes and other great healing shrines.

Below:
Flint Castle. One of the lesser-known of Edward I's castles, Flint is at the north-eastern corner of Wales, on the shore of the Dee estuary.

lived in by the Myddelton family.
• Just inside Wales, off the A5, some seven miles east of Llangollen.
Phone: 01691 777701
www.nationaltrust.org.uk

Corwen

Rug Chapel and Llangar Church. These delightful religious buildings will take you back to another age. Rug is a rare example of a little-altered private chapel of the 17th century. Its exterior is plain but inside – from the pew ends to the amazing roof – the skills of local woodcarvers and artists were given free rein. Llangar Church, in contrast, is a medieval building with 15th century wall paintings and a minstrels' gallery. It was remodelled in the early 18th century.
• Close together near Corwen. Rug is a mile to the north-west on the A494, and Llangar is a mile to the south-west on the B4401.
www.llangollen.com

Denbigh

Denbigh Castle. Crowning the steep hill above the town, Denbigh Castle, along with the mighty gatehouse below and the encircling town walls, was put up by Henry de Lacy, Earl of Lincoln, one of Edward I's commanders during his late-13th century campaigns against the Welsh. There are panoramic views of the Vale of Clwyd from the castle and its ramparts.
• There is parking space at the castle; the lower gatehouse is amid narrow residential streets.
Phone: 01745 813385
www.cadw.wales.gov.uk

Theatr Twm o'r Nant, Denbigh. Community productions, particularly in the Welsh language, are the staple of this thriving theatre in Denbigh. It also hosts public talks and recordings of BBC radio programmes, as well as meetings and rehearsals of local choirs, groups and societies. Its programme is typical of the ferment of cultural activity that goes on

every week throughout Wales.
• Details from Denbigh Library and local bookshops.
Phone: 01745 550374
www.visitdenbigh.co.uk

HM Stanley Exhibition, Denbigh. Explorer, journalist and author Henry Morton Stanley overcame a harsh childhood as an orphan in Denbigh, to achieve fame and many honours in Britain and the USA. His finest hour came when he fulfiled a commission from the 'New York Herald' to find the Victorian explorer David Livingstone, who was presumed lost in the depths of Africa. When he found him, Stanley uttered the immortal words "Doctor Livingstone, I presume..."
• Items are on display at Denbigh Library and Museum.
www.visitdenbigh.co.uk

Flint

Flint Castle. Built following the Welsh campaigns of Edward I in 1277, Flint is one of his lesser-known castles. Standing solidly on the shore of the Dee estuary, it reflects the importance of secure access to and from the sea, as do many castles around Wales. This is where Richard II was held in 1399 before he was dethroned and replaced as king by Henry IV.
• On the Dee estuary coast between Connah's Quay and Holywell.
www.cadw.wales.co.uk

Greenfield Valley

Step back in time as you walk through this attractive country park, where birdsong and the scents of wild flowers have replaced the cacophony and noxious fumes of the copper smelting works that once stood here. At the museum and farm, reconstructed buildings contain agricultural displays, a working smithy and farm animals.
• From J32 on the A55, follow signs to Greenfield Valley.
Phone: 01352 714172
www.greenfieldvalley.com

Left:
Basingwerk Abbey.
Unlike many medieval abbeys, Basingwerk was within reach of centres of population and the monks there made a good living from the agricultural produce they sold locally.

Below:
Llangollen Canal.
Relaxing horse-drawn boat trips along the scenic Llangollen Canal offer great views over the town and to the surrounding hills.

Basingwerk Abbey. Less remote than most other monasteries of the the Cistercian order, the picturesque ruins of 12th century Basingwerk Abbey are to be found in the **Greenfield Valley Heritage Park**. The monastic community here was renowned for its hospitality to visitors. Traveller and writer Gerald of Wales came here in 1188 and Edward I stayed here whilst building Flint Castle in the 13th century. The monks profited from trading in wool, salt, lead and silver. Pilgrims thronging to nearby St Winefride's Well, which was in the care of the abbey, brought additional prosperity. The abbey was dissolved in 1536 by Henry VIII. Only a little of the 12th century walling survives and much of what is visible today, including the church, dates from the early 13th century when the buildings were generally refurbished and extended. The attractions of the Greenfield Valley make a marvellously varied walk.
www.cadw.wales.gov.uk

....

Hawarden

St Deiniol's Library. Britain's only residential library was founded by the great Victorian statesman and four-times Prime Minister, William Ewart Gladstone. Following his death in 1898, it became the nation's memorial to his life and work. A voracious reader and collector of books, he assembled a remarkable collection reflecting his many interests. This has since grown to more than 200,000 volumes on history, theology, philosophy, the classics, art and literature.
• St Deiniol's Library is in Hawarden, just north of the A55 at J35, along the A550.
Phone: 01244 532350
www.st-deiniols.co.uk

....

Holywell

St Winefride's Well. This most famous of all of the holy wells of Wales has been in continuous use as a place of healing since medieval times. King Henry V walked here from Shrewsbury, to give thanks for victory at Agincourt. The elaborate vaulted chapel over the well was built in around 1500, at the instigation of Margaret Beaufort, mother of Henry VII. King James II and his wife Mary came here in 1686 to pray, successfully, for a son. The beautiful statue of St Winefride and the calm environs of the shrine and the nearby church enhance the deep spiritual significance of this remarkable place, where pilgrims still come to bathe in the healing waters.
• Down the hill from Holywell town centre. There is a car park at a respectful distance, from which it is but a short walk to the well.
Phone: 01352 713054
www.saintwinefrideswell.com

Pantasaph Friary. This Franciscan friary welcomes visitors who are keen to learn more about Catholic spirituality. It is home to the national **shrine of St Pio**, operates as a retreat centre and offers an uplifting walk around an outdoor representation of the Stations of the Cross.
• Immediately west of Holywell – accessible from J31 and J32 of the A55.

....

Llangollen

Few towns anywhere enjoy a more picturesque location. Framed by green hills, one of them topped by the ruins of **Castell Dinas Brân**, and with the river Dee rushing under its fine stone bridge, the town is a delightful place to explore.
• From the several car parks, follow the comprehensively signed walking routes along the river bank and around the town.
www.borderlands.co.uk
For details of Llangollen International Musical Eisteddfod see page 61.

Llangollen Canal. This is generally agreed among canal-cruising folk to be the most beautiful canal in the UK. It extends some forty miles westward from the Shropshire Union canal, which is a pleasant three-day cruise for a narrowboat, and enters Wales in the most spectacular fashion possible, crossing high above the Dee valley on the Chirk and Pontcysyllte aqueducts.
• There are horse-drawn boat trips if you

Left:
Llangollen Steam Railway. This is the spectacular point where the Llangollen Steam Railway runs high above the river Dee, west of the town, opposite the Chain Bridge Hotel.

Below:
Plas Newydd. William Wordsworth, Sir Walter Scott and the Duke of Wellington were among the luminaries who visited the Ladies of Llangollen at their Gothically furnished and decorated home, Plas Newydd.

would like a brief introduction to the canal's delights.
www.waterscape.com

Llangollen Steam Railway. This scenic section of the Ruabon to Barmouth railway line closed to passengers in 1965 and to goods in 1968, when the tracks and signalling were removed. A keen group of volunteers has since reinstated several miles of track along the **Dee valley** towards Corwen. Trains operate at weekends for most of the year, and daily from June to October. It is a joy to hear the tooting of the trains and to savour the atmosphere of the old station as sunlight slants through the smoke and steam. Regular events include **steam galas** with visiting engines, appearances by Thomas the Tank Engine, and Santa Specials.
• The station is just across the bridge from the town centre.
www.llangollen-railway.co.uk

Llangollen Motor Museum. Take a trip down memory lane to see the cars and motorbikes that your grandparents' generation used to drive. Remember – or perhaps encounter for the first time – double de-clutching, starting handles, semaphore indicators and the evocative smell of old leather upholstery. See how the village mechanic and his wife lived and worked, and the tools he used. History is fun at Llangollen Motor Museum, and the shop has gifts, books and even some spare parts for older cars.
• Between the canal and the river, just over a mile westward from the bridge towards the Horseshoe Pass.
Phone: 01978 860324
www.llangollenmotormuseum.co.uk

The Chapel – Y Capel Art Gallery.
Conveniently situated near the centre of Llangollen, this gallery in a former chapel aims high, and features changing exhibitions of paintings, prints and ceramics, ranging from landscape to abstract work, by some of the leading

artists of Wales.
Phone: 01978 860828

Castell Dinas Brân. A vigorous walk up the well-marked path from Llangollen to the ruins of Castell Dinas Brân brings wonderful rewards in the form of 360 degree panoramas of the town, the **Dee valley, Eglwyseg Mountain** and **the Horseshoe Pass.** Occupied by its original Welsh builders for only a few decades, the castle was attacked by the forces of Edward I in 1277, and has remained in ruins ever since. Wordsworth was moved to lament its fate with the words: 'Relic of kings, wreck of forgotten wars. To the winds abandoned and the prying stars.'
• The Tourist Information Centre and local shops have maps and guidebooks describing walks and cycle routes.
Phone: 01352 810614
www.denbighshire.gov.uk

Plas Newydd. This timbered mansion was home to the Ladies of Llangollen – the Irish aristocrats Eleanor Butler and Sarah Ponsonby – who settled here and entertained countless society and literary figures during the early decades of the 19th century. Plas Newydd is set in peaceful gardens surrounded by trees and contains the font from the nearby Valle Crucis Abbey. The house is now a museum run by Denbighshire County Council. The circle of stones in the grounds of Plas Newydd were used for the 1908 Llangollen National Eisteddfod.
• Walk up the main street, away from the river, and carefully cross the A5 at the top; head left, then right up a residential road, to nearby Plas Newydd.
Phone: 01978 861314
www.borderlands.co.uk

Valle Crucis Abbey. One of the most attractively situated of Wales's sacred places, Valle Crucis takes its name – Vale of the Cross – from the beautiful valley near Llangollen where a 9th century cross, the Pillar of Eliseg, stands. Founded in

1201 by the local Welsh ruler, Madoc ap Gruffydd Maelor, whose family later built the hilltop fortress of Dinas Brân, the abbey conformed to the rules of the white-robed Cistercians, which stated that their monasteries should be built "far from the haunts of men".

• Between Llangollen and the spectacular Horseshoe Pass, on the A542.
www.cadw.wales.gov.uk

Mold

This pleasing market town is the birthplace of Daniel Owen, one of the finest novelists in the Welsh language. The museum above the library chronicles his life and introduces the much-loved characters in the novels he produced during the late 19th century. The compact town centre has family-run shops among familiar high street names. The bustling street market, popular since the 17th century, extends from the square towards the parish church every Wednesday and Saturday.

• Signed from the A55 and from Wrexham.
www.borderlands.co.uk

Clwyd Theatr Cymru. This highly acclaimed centre of theatrical excellence, standing on the hill above Mold, is home to Wales's major drama-producing theatre company. Under the inspired leadership of director Terry Hands, the actors and technicians achieve production standards that are second to none. The company regularly presents its work on tour throughout Wales, and the theatre also hosts visiting productions, concerts, and exhibitions.

• Drive up past the council offices to the car parks in front of the theatre.
Phone: 01352 756331
www.clwyd-theatr-cymru.co.uk

Rhuddlan

This was yet another of the castles built by Edward I. He issued the Statute of Rhuddlan here in 1284, imposing English legal and administrative systems on the territories he had seized. The castle's most remarkable attribute is the means by which ships were able to bring supplies to its river gate, some three miles from the sea. In a mammoth exercise involving hundreds of workers, the River Clwyd was deepened and straightened to make a canal.

• A couple of miles north of St Asaph, from J27 on the A55 expressway.
Phone: 01745 590777
www.cadw.wales.co.uk

Ruthin

There are some remarkable listed buildings around the town square of Ruthin. Several of the half-timbered buildings, now occupied by banks and shops, have been in business since medieval times. **St Peter's Church** was the first to be built in the spacious double-naved style found in this part of the UK. Look for the "Eyes of Ruthin", the distinctive dormer windows in the roof of the **Castle Hotel** on the square.

• All approaches give wide views of the broad Vale of Clwyd.
www.borderlands.co.uk

Ruthin Castle. A succession of owners since medieval times enlarged this fortified site. In 1826, a fine house was built over part of the castle and was later extended. Ruthin Castle is now a hotel and conference centre; it has become famous for its medieval-style Welsh banquets, with traditional food, drink and entertainment.

• A short drive or walk along a narrow road leading from the main town square.
Phone: 01824 702664
www.ruthincastle.co.uk

Ruthin Gaol. The stout walls and barred windows of Ruthin Gaol still exude a daunting presence, though you may visit nowadays and tour the interior, including the condemned man's cell, with the certainty of getting out again.

• A short walk down the hill from Ruthin's ancient main square.

Right:
Valle Crucis Abbey. A short distance north of Llangollen, on the way to the dramatic Horseshoe Pass, Valle Crucis Abbey graces a sylvan valley of great beauty.

Left:
Erddig Hall.
Elaborate 18th century gardens and sumptuous interiors are testimony to the no-expense-spared approach to materials and workmanship at this fine country house.

Below:
St Asaph Cathedral. Destroyed by the soldiers of Henry III in 1245 and by the armies of Edward I in 1282, St Asaph Cathedral was substantially rebuilt between 1284 and 1381 only to be burned by Owain Glyndŵr's Welsh troops in 1402. The existing building is largely 14th century with many Victorian alterations.

Ruthin Craft Centre. This purpose-built craft centre has two exhibition galleries displaying a changing programme of contemporary applied art. There is a shop and a pleasant restaurant, as well as independent workshops accommodating designer-craftworkers whose activities include glass blowing, ceramics, textiles, fine art prints and jewellery.
• On the edge of the town centre, with parking available.
Phone: 01824 703992
www.borderlands.co.uk

St Asaph

St Asaph Cathedral. This is the mother church of the diocese of St Asaph, one of the six dioceses of the Church in Wales. The Celtic saint Kentigern built his original church here in 560 AD. When he returned to Strathclyde in 573 AD he left Asaph as his successor, and the cathedral has been dedicated to St Asaph since that time. The present building was begun in the 13th century and is generally agreed to be the smallest cathedral in the UK. Its bishops have included the Norman writer and historian Geoffrey of Monmouth and Bishop William Morgan, who translated the Bible into Welsh.
• Within sight of the A55 – exit at J27.
Phone: 01745 583429
www.stasaphcathedral.org.uk

Trelawnyd

Gop cairn at Trelawnyd. The enormous mound on Gop Hill is the biggest prehistoric monument in Wales and the second largest in all Britain, outmatched only by Silbury Hill near Avebury. Standing 46 feet (14m) tall, and some 820 feet (250m) above sea level, the limestone blocks used to build the great oval mound are plain to see. It is usually given a late-Neolithic origin, somewhere around 3,000 BC, but the purpose for which it was so laboriously built is shrouded in mystery. As with similar monuments, possibilities include an astronomical viewing platform, a focus for rituals connected with sun worship, a monument to the dead, or a massive burial mound.
• Five miles eastward from Rhuddlan, on the A5151.

Wrexham

As the largest town in north Wales, Wrexham is a busy commercial and administrative centre with all of the educational, cultural, sports and leisure resources you would expect. Its origins as a market town are preserved in the half-timbered building of the town centre and the three excellent indoor markets.
• The town centre is pedestrianised and suitably compact for exploration on foot.
www.wrexham.gov.uk

Wrexham Arts Centre. The Centre has two galleries, organises touring exhibitions and is a popular venue for art classes, lectures and school visits. In association with the **Yale Memorial Gallery** – at Yale College – it has organised, exhibited and toured successful international print exhibitions. **The Regional Print Centre** provides print-making facilities to artists and the public, for monotype, etching, relief and screenprinting on paper, textiles, ceramics and glass.
• If you are unfamiliar with this largest of north-Wales towns, a detailed map or visitor guide will come in handy.
Phone: 01978 292093 (Arts Centre)
Phone: 01978 311794 (Gallery/Print Centre)

Erddig Hall. Here, in one of the most fascinating historic houses in the UK, you will experience something of the intertwined lives of a family and its servants. The former occupied the outstandingly beautiful staterooms, with their fine 18th and 19th century furniture and decor, including some exquisite Chinese wallpaper. The latter worked away in the kitchen, bakehouse, laundry, stables, smithy and sawmill. The large walled garden has been restored to its formal 18th century glory and contains the national

Above:
St Giles Church.
Dedicated to the
busy patron saint
of beggars,
blacksmiths,
Edinburgh, hermits,
horses, disabled
people and many
other causes.

Top left:
'The Arc', a
dramatic sculpture
in Wrexham's town
centre,
commemorates
the miners and
steelworkers of
the area.

Left:
Wrexham's markets
offer a wide range
of appealing
produce from Wales
and further afield.

collection of ivy varieties.
• Prominently signed from the main
approaches to Wrexham from the south.
Phone: 01978 355314
www.nationaltrust.org.uk

St Giles's Church. The massive tower of
St Giles's Wrexham dominates the town's
skyline and is justly numbered among the
"Seven Wonders of Wales". Richly decorated
and pinnacled, it stands 147 feet (45 metres)
high. It has a twin across the Atlantic – a
replica built in the 1920s at Yale University
to honour that institution's benefactor,
Elihu Yale of Wrexham, who lies buried only
a few feet from St Giles's tower.
• There is a large car park immediately
below the elevated site of the church.
Phone: 01978 355808
www.wrexham.gov.uk

Gallery 103 at NEWI. The North East Wales
Institute of Higher Education, part of the
University of Wales, opened its Gallery 103
in 2002. It quickly proved an asset to the

local community, displaying works by a
wide range of internationally famous
artists, along with the work of NEWI's art
students, in exhibitions that change
throughout the year. The William Aston
Hall, also part of NEWI, accommodates
musical performances and public lectures.
Phone: 01978 290666 www.newi.ac.uk

Clywedog Valley. Wrexham's industrial
heritage is dramatically preserved at the
**Bersham Heritage Centre Iron Works and
Minera Lead Mines**. Follow the fascinating
Clywedog Valley trail and call at the **Nant
Mill Visitor Centre** to learn about the
area's contribution to the Industrial
Revolution.
• Five miles west of Wrexham on the A525,
or carefully navigate the remote and
narrow mountain road from Llangollen
via World's End.
Phone: 01978 261529 (Bersham
Heritage Centre) Phone: 01978 752772
(Nant Mill Visitor Centre)
www.wrexham.gov.uk

Left:
Llangollen International Musical Eisteddfod. Hundreds of colourfully costumed competitors travel from all over the world to enjoy the camaraderie and high performance standards of the Llangollen International Musical Eisteddfod.

Rhosllanerchrugog Miners' Institute. Culture and education were given high priority in the mining and quarrying communities of Wales. Institutes such as this housed the theatres, meeting rooms and libraries in which the miners and their families elevated their thoughts from the harshness of the pit. **The Stiwt**, restored to its considerable former glory, combines a state-of-the-art theatre with a multi-purpose Welsh cultural centre, befitting its place at the heart of a talented community with deep and long-standing cultural traditions.
• Often described as Wales's largest village, Rhosllanerchrugog is on the B5097 south-west of Wrexham.
Phone: 01978 844053
www.stiwt.co.uk

Festivals and events

Flintshire Festival. October is the time to enjoy this well-established mix of music, dance and drama, along with interesting guided walks and talks during which you will learn about the history and culture of this north-eastern corner of Wales.
www.flintshire.gov.uk

Gŵyl Cadi Ha – folk dancing. Traditional Welsh folk dancing ranges from the athletic clog dances enjoyed by off-duty farm workers in centuries past to the sedate formations practised by the gentry in the grand houses. The colourful costumes and precision steps are revived at this celebration at the beginning of **May**, led by the mischievous figure of Cadi Ha' and echoing seasonal celebrations dating back to pagan times.
• A roving event in the vicinity of Holywell, the Greenfield Valley and Mold.
Phone: 01352 755614

Llangollen International Musical Eisteddfod. This wonderful celebration of diverse cultures was founded as a means of bringing nations together and healing the scars left by the Second World War. Musicians and dancers from all over the world travel to Llangollen in early **July** to enjoy the atmosphere of friendly competition and the warm welcome extended by the town. Evening concerts feature big names from classical music, opera, world music and musical theatre.
• The Llangollen International Pavilion is within walking distance of the town centre, across the bridge and to the left.
Phone: 01978 862000
www.international-eisteddfod.co.uk

North Wales International Jazz Guitar Festival. The organisers reckon, with considerable justification, that this is the biggest and most exciting event of its kind in the world. It features the cream of jazz guitarists from the UK and the rest of Europe, along with visiting luminaries from the USA.
• Held in **August** at venues in and around Wrexham.
Phone: 01745 812260
www.northwalesjazz.org.uk

North Wales International Music Festival. The attractive cathedral of St Asaph is the main venue for this festival held every **September**. Orchestral, choral and chamber music is performed by musicians of the highest calibre. The festival is a legacy of the eminent Welsh composer William Mathias, who is buried in the shade of the cathedral and its surrounding trees.
• Programme from local libraries and Tourist Information Centres, or link from the Arts Council of Wales website.
Phone: 01745 584508
www.northwalesmuscifestival.co.uk

Denbigh Midsummer Festival. This week long festival of music, drama, exhibitions and poetry is held in mid **June** in this historic town in the beautiful Vale of Clwyd, which has performance venues of great character.
• Details from Denbigh Library, local shops and hotels.
Phone: 01745 814646
www.visitdenbigh.co.uk

Snowdonia Mountains and Coast

Caernarfon Castle, Tŷ Mawr Wybrnant, Llanrwst, several narrow-gauge railways, Bardsey Island and Portmeirion.
The National Slate Museum, Nant Gwrtheyrn, and Bryn Terfel's Faenol Festival are cultural treasures.

Above:
Snowdon Horseshoe.
Wales's highest mountain might appear to be pristine wilderness but hill farmers, slate quarrymen and copper miners have all earned a living on its slopes – and a small hydro-electric power station puts the high rainfall generated by the mountain to productive use.

Bangor

Penrhyn Castle. In an ostentatious display of the wealth he and his family had extracted from their slate quarries at Bethesda, George Dawkins (who adopted the family name Pennant) built this grandiose mock-Norman mansion near Port Penrhyn, the harbour from which the slate was exported. Queen Victoria famously declined to sleep in the giant slate four-poster bed made especially for her visit to the area.

• Just outside Bangor – leave the A55 at J11 or J12.
Phone: 01248 353084
www.nationaltrust.org.uk

Bardsey Island

The holy island of Bardsey exudes a mystical presence among the racing tides off the tip of the Llŷn peninsula. The tower of the 13th century **St Mary's Abbey**, which was the goal of countless medieval pilgrims, remains standing amid the ruins of the Augustinian monastery. Merlin the Magician – Myrddin Emrys, to give him his Welsh name – is said to be buried there, along with 20,000 saints. Visits are regulated by the Bardsey Island Trust. Many people each year find that a day spent there, or a longer retreat, can be a spiritually uplifting experience.

• There are spectacular vistas of Bardsey from the minor roads above Aberdaron.

Pilgrim's Route to Bardsey. By means of arcane spiritual arithmetic, the medieval Catholic Church calculated that three pilgrimages to the holy island of Bardsey equalled one to Rome. But it was not an easy option: the pilgrims had to make their way to the far-western tip of the Llŷn peninsula, then endure the two mile crossing of the often turbulent sound. An early glimmer of a tourism industry catered for their needs, providing accommodation and food, and water from wells on the way.

• Enquire at local Tourist Information Centres or churches for a map to enable you to follow their route.

Beddgelert

Sygun Copper Mine. Snowdonia is riddled with mine workings: gold, silver, lead, copper and other minerals have been found here over the centuries. Sygun's mine galleries extend deep into the mountain, and an audio commentary describes the lives of the miners. The **Red Dragon Heritage Centre** tells how the Welsh flag was inspired by the legend of the red dragon of Wales defeating the white dragon of the Saxons in the presence of Merlin the Magician, a defeat that occurred at Dinas Emrys, the rocky outcrop across the valley.

• North-east of Beddgelert, on the A498 towards Capel Curig.
Phone: 01766 890595
www.syguncoppermine.co.uk

Betws-y-coed

Dolwyddelan Castle. This sentinel, deep in the heart of Snowdonia, is one of several castles built by Llywelyn the Great. The stark square tower, visible for miles around, guarded the strategic pass linking Meirionydd in the south of his kingdom and Conwy in the north. The mildly strenuous walk up to the castle from the car park is very worthwhile for the panoramic mountain vistas.

• Between Betws-y-coed and Blaenau Ffestiniog, on the A470.
Phone: 01690 750366
www.cadw.wales.gov.uk

Tŷ Mawr Wybrnant. Small but significant, this is the birthplace of Bishop William Morgan who, in 1588, translated the Bible into Welsh. By doing so, he made the hearing and reading of exemplary Welsh accessible to all, thus securing the status and future of the language. This National Trust property, in the beautiful and

Above left:
Cwm Croesor. Thousands of workers once laboured in the slate quarries and mines of Bethesda, Llanberis, Blaenau Ffestiniog and Corris.

Above:
Sygun Copper Mine. Visitors can discover for themselves the wonders of Sygun - the winding tunnels, large chambers, magnificent stalactites and stalagmites and copper ore veins - just as it was when it was abandoned in 1903.

Above:
Caernarfon Castle.
The imposing scale of Caernarfon Castle is evident from the river Seiont quayside, or from the other side of the River, across the footbridge.

secluded **Wybrnant valley** near Penmachno, has been restored to its likely appearance in the 16th century. A woodland walk takes you past traditionally managed fields, where William Morgan's family once farmed.
• Signed from the A5 just south-east of Betws-y-coed, along the B4406 to Penmachno.
Phone: 01690 760213
www.nationaltrust.org.uk

Blaenau Ffestiniog

Llechwedd Slate Caverns. For a thought-provoking insight into the harsh life of the quarrymen, take the underground train journey at Llechwedd to see where they spent their long working days. We are privileged to be able to enjoy the beautiful rock formations and underground lakes of this deep slate mine without the noise, dust and danger that was involved in extracting the slate and bringing it to the surface.
• Just north of Blaenau Ffestiniog on the A470.

Phone: 01766 830306
www.llechwedd-slate-caverns.co.uk

Caernarfon

The castle is just one of many attractions in Caernarfon, the county town of Gwynedd. Substantial Victorian buildings, including the imposing **County Hall** and the **Harbour Office** on the quay, lend their purposeful presence. The sympathetic architecture of **Gwynedd Council's** modern headquarters sits comfortably amongst the narrow streets in the shadow of the castle.
A dynamic sculpture of David Lloyd George appears to be giving a rousing speech over Y Maes, the central square. The steam trains of the **Welsh Highland Railway** head into Snowdonia from the Slate Quay.
• Enjoy exploring the historic streets on foot, and revive yourself at one of the numerous cafés.

Caernarfon – Victoria Dock. The maritime museum at Victoria Dock tells the story of

this fascinating port, including its growth during the 19th century as it became an important centre for the export of slate quarried in the mountains. On the quayside is **Galeri,** Caernarfon's thriving arts centre, with its excellent performance spaces complemented by offices and rehearsal rooms for numerous arts organisations. **Gwynedd's county archives,** which contain a treasure trove of historical material, are nearby.
• Just outside the town walls, with limited parking near the museum and ample parking (and a pleasant café) at Galeri.

Caernarfon Castle. The largest of the castles built by Edward I in his attempt to control this corner of Wales dominates the town that has grown around it. It stands at the confluence of the River Seiont and the Menai Strait, near the **Roman fort of Segontium**. Its polygonal towers and contrasting bands of masonry imitate the walls of Constantinople. It echoes the legendary dream of the Roman general Magnus Maximus, defender of north-western Britannia, who saw a vision of a beautiful woman in a distant castle and was said to have found her here. Edward knowingly played on these associations when, in his determination to show his strength, he built this overwhelming symbol of his power.
• From the large car park on the quay, walk round to the entrance at the inland side of the castle.
Phone: 01286 677617
www.cadw.wales.gov.uk

Roman fort – Segontium. This base for a regiment of around a thousand infantry, which also served as an administrative centre for the collection of taxes, was founded by Agricola in 77 AD, after he had finally conquered the local Celtic tribe, the Ordovices. The on-site museum has impressive finds from the extensive archaeological excavations that revealed the fort, barracks and stores, and the adjacent temple of Mithras.

• At the edge of town, on the A4085 towards Beddgelert.
Phone: 01286 675625
www.segontium.org.uk

Inigo Jones Slate Works. Slate, which varies in colour from bluish-purple to grey or green, is a wonderfully versatile resource. It is a multi-purpose building material, usable in thin layers for roofing and cladding, and in greater bulk for walls and paths. It can resist all that the weather might throw at it and lasts for many centuries. It is also capable of being intricately shaped into jewellery and decorative items, and is used, finely ground, in cosmetics. Here, at one of the region's smaller slate quarries, you will find a workshop producing a wide range of attractive items, both functional and artistic.
• Off the A487, some five miles south of Caernarfon.
Phone: 01286 830242
www.inigojones.co.uk

Corris

King Arthur's Labyrinth, Corris. Wales has many sites associated with King Arthur, whose legends are likely to have grown from the real-life exploits of a Celtic chieftain (or perhaps several of them) who emerged after the departure of the Romans. The tales are re-told in dramatic underground settings at King Arthur's Labyrinth near Corris in southern Snowdonia.
• Between Dolgellau and Machynlleth, on the A487.
Phone: 01654 761584
www.kingarthurslabyrinth.com

Criccieth

Criccieth Castle. Originally a stronghold of the Welsh princes with a gatehouse built by Llywelyn the Great between 1230 and 1240, Criccieth Castle fell to Edward I in 1283. It was captured and burned by Owain Glyndŵr in 1404. The walls still bear

evidence of scorching from that attack. Dramatically situated on a headland between two beaches, it has inspired countless artists, including JMW Turner.
• Head westward from Porthmadog towards Pwllheli (A497). Your first sighting of the castle guarding the bay will be memorable.
Phone: 01766 522227
www.cadw.wales.gov.uk

Harlech

Harlech Castle. With the sea on one side of its cliff-top location, the tough terrain of Snowdonia on the other, and a massive gatehouse guarding its landward side, Harlech Castle would have been a tough nut to crack for any attacker. Built in the late 13th century, as Edward I's stronghold in southern Gwynedd, it was occupied by Welsh revolutionary Owain Glyndŵr in 1404. A long siege there during the Wars of the Roses inspired the stirring song "Men of Harlech".
• From Porthmadog, a small toll to use the minor road across the estuary saves several miles of driving.
Phone: 01766 780552
www.cadw.wales.gov.uk

Llanberis

Dolbadarn Castle. Presiding over Llyn Padarn, at the foot of Snowdon, this is one of the most magnificently situated castles built by the Welsh princes. It guarded the approach to the highest pass through Snowdonia, linking Caernarfon and the Conwy valley. It has been a popular subject for landscape painters since the pioneering visits by the great Welsh artist Richard Wilson. Several atmospheric studies were produced here, in both oils and watercolour, by JMW Turner, one of which he submitted as his Diploma work to the Royal Academy.
• There is a car park just along the road to the National Slate Museum, and a footpath leads through woodland to the castle.
www.cadw.wales.gov.uk

National Slate Museum. Llanberis was a major centre of the slate-quarrying industry that once employed thousands in this corner of Wales. The tough working conditions and the camaraderie of the quarry community are brought to life in the original working buildings and terraced cottages preserved at the National Slate Museum, a National Museum Wales site. Former quarrymen demonstrate the skills required to split and trim this remarkable layered rock to make roofing slates and decorative items.
• Off the A4086 at Llanberis.
Phone: 01286 870630
www.museumwales.ac.uk

Llanrwst

With its historic centre little changed for four hundred years, this attractive market town serves the surrounding Conwy valley. The hump-backed stone bridge (take care as you cross) was reputedly designed by the famous landscape architect Inigo Jones and dates from 1636. The Almshouses, built in 1610, are now a community museum, with an attractive herb garden. Llanrwst considers itself independent of the UK and has its own flag and arms. It once applied (unsuccessfully) for membership of the United Nations!
• Ten miles south of the A55 (J19) and five miles north of Betws-y-coed, on the A470.

Gwydir Castle. Built for the Wynn family in around 1500, this handsome Tudor courtyard house, with peacocks strutting around the Grade I listed formal gardens, has been skilfully restored by its owners. Their efforts included retrieving panelling and carvings that had been removed and taken elsewhere – in the case of the panelled dining room from the 1640s, to New York's Metropolitan Museum. Gwydir has a reputation for being one of the most haunted houses in Wales.
• A short drive or a pleasant walk to the opposite side of the River Conwy from Llanrwst.
Phone: 01492 641687
www.gwydircastle.co.uk

**Left:
Portmeirion.** Pleasingly composed vistas – through arches, between buildings, along lanes and across the colourful gardens – appear at every turn as you wander the delightful grounds.

Nant Gwrtheyrn

The isolated coastal quarry village of Nant Gwrtheyrn, reached by descending one of the steepest roads in Wales, is now the popular **Welsh Language and Heritage Centre**. In this inspirational location, many people each year learn to speak Welsh on five-day or twelve-day residential courses, or explore Wales's fascinating history. It is also a great place for a brief visit, perhaps including a meal at the restaurant, or a self-catering holiday.

• Follow signs from Llithfaen, on the B4417 north-east of Nefyn – and take great care descending the hill.
Phone: 01758 750334
www.nantgwrtheyrn.org

Portmeirion

Architect Sir Clough Williams-Ellis described his wonderfully eclectic fantasy village as his "Home for Fallen Buildings". This cornucopia of piazzas, colonnades, domes and arches, enlivened by a riot of fountains, ornate gateways, belvederes, statues and flower borders, depends for its effect on his gift for arranging vistas, perspective and focal points into a most pleasing whole. Portmeirion is generally Italian in style, though there are numerous buildings and features saved from demolition in Wales and elsewhere. Fans of the television series The Prisoner visit to see where their hero tried so hard to escape from the Village. The **Portmeirion and Castell Deudraeth hotels**, both within the estate, are great places to stay or to enjoy a meal.

• Prominently signed at Minffordd, between Porthmadog and Penrhyndeudraeth to the east.
Phone: 01766 770228
www.portmeirion-village.com

Rhiw

Plas yn Rhiw. This small 16th century manor house, which has Georgian additions, was rescued from neglect and lovingly restored by the three Keating sisters, who bought it in 1938. The views of Cardigan Bay are spectacular.
The delightful ornamental garden has box hedges and grass paths, and is a riot of flowering trees and shrubs in summer.

• Carefully negotiate the minor roads between Abersoch and Aberdaron at the extremity of the Llŷn peninsula.
Phone: 01758 780219
www.nationaltrust.org.uk

Tre'r Ceiri

Iron Age fort at Tre'r Ceiri. The Celtic people who lived in Britain before the arrival of the Romans usually built their settlements on easily defended hilltops or narrow coastal promontories. Tre'r Ceiri – Town of the Giants – occupies a spectacular position crowning one of the sharp peaks of The Rivals, with uninterrupted views in all directions. A three-metre-high wall surrounds some 150 stone hut bases, making this a community of considerable size.

• Close to Llanaelhaearn, fourteen miles south-west of Caernarfon on the A499. The climb to Tre'r Ceiri is strenuous.

Tywyn

Castell y Bere. The southernmost of the castles of the kingdom of Gwynedd stands near the border with Ceredigion on a rocky outcrop on the floor of the **Dysynni valley**, where a well provided fresh water. The layout of the interior, including the royal apartments, is clearly preserved, and it is easy to imagine Prince Llywelyn the Great, who built it, enjoying peaceful times here with his family and court.

• The B4405 and the Talyllyn narrow-gauge railway head up the Dysynni valley from Tywyn to Abergynolwyn. A minor road leads to the castle.
www.cadw.wales.gov.uk

Railways. Nothing quite matches the atmosphere of a trip on a steam train as it rattles over the points and chuffs along

Left:
Bryn Terfel's Faenol Festival. Combines musical excellence with the most scenic of surroundings.

through the countryside, the experience intensified by that evocative bouquet of smoke, soot and hot oil. The **Ffestiniog, Welsh Highland, Snowdon, Padarn Lake, Talyllyn and Bala Lake railways** provide an escape from the car and a great way of enjoying the view. Some lines have industrial origins: the **Ffestiniog Railway** was built to bring slate down from the quarries to ships at Porthmadog. Others are purely scenic: the **Snowdon Railway** has carried passengers to the summit of Wales's highest mountain since 1896.
• Timetables and details from Tourist Information Centres.
www.visitwales.com

Festivals and events

Abersoch Jazz Festival. The seaside village of Abersoch echoes to the sounds of jazz, including both indoor and outdoor performances, during early **June** each year. Famous names and local musicians; street music and a colourful parade; competitions, stalls and a gospel music service all maintain the international flavour of this popular festival.
• For Abersoch, follow the A497 and A499 from Porthmadog and Pwllheli.
www.abersochjazzfestival.com

Bryn Terfel's Faenol Festival. When the internationally renowned bass-baritone Bryn Terfel, who was born in Snowdonia and now lives near Caernarfon, decided to give something back to the community that nurtured his outstanding musical abilities, he did not do so half-heartedly. Each year, he invites some of the biggest stars of opera, musical theatre, rock and Welsh popular music to join him on stage at his four day festival. This musical feast of the highest order, held over the **August** bank-holiday weekend, enjoys a spectacular location at the Faenol Estate near Bangor, with Snowdonia as a backdrop, and has been voted the Best Show in Wales.
• The Faenol Estate is just west of Bangor, close to J9 on the A55 expressway.
Phone: 01286 672232 (TIC)
www.brynfest.com

Criccieth Festival. Mid **June** finds this most picturesque of seaside towns buzzing with musical and literary activity. Classical musicians, Welsh choirs, singers and dancers, and visiting performers from overseas bring a wonderful variety of styles to the town's fine Memorial Hall and other venues. Other highlights include fascinating talks, including the **David Lloyd George Memorial Lecture**, garden visits and a family fun day with fireworks.
• Criccieth is on the A497 and is also well served by train services between Porthmadog and Pwllheli.
Phone: 01766 522778
www.cricciethfestival.co.uk

Gwyl Bwyd Môr Llŷn Seafood Festival. This annual seafood festival promises to be 'an assault on the tastebuds'. Held at Pwllheli Marina over a weekend in early **July**, it displays the culinary riches of the sea as well as other locally produced Welsh foods. The festival involves tastings, cookery demonstrations and lectures where visitors can learn about the art of cooking seafood from celebrity chefs. The festival is organised by the Llŷn Fishermen's Association.
• Pwllheli is just off the A499 and is also served by regular trains.
Phone: 01758 720656

Sesiwn Fawr Dolgellau. The "Big Session" in **July** has outgrown its former home on the town square. Nowadays its five main stages occupy the Marian, the area of car parks and playing fields on the riverbank near the bridge. Expect to be part of a large and enthusiastic crowd as you enjoy performances by established world music, rock and folk bands from Wales, Ireland and far beyond, including strong representation from the thriving Welsh-language music scene.
• The town is signed from the A470 and A494.
Phone: 08712 301314
www.sesiwnfawr.co.uk

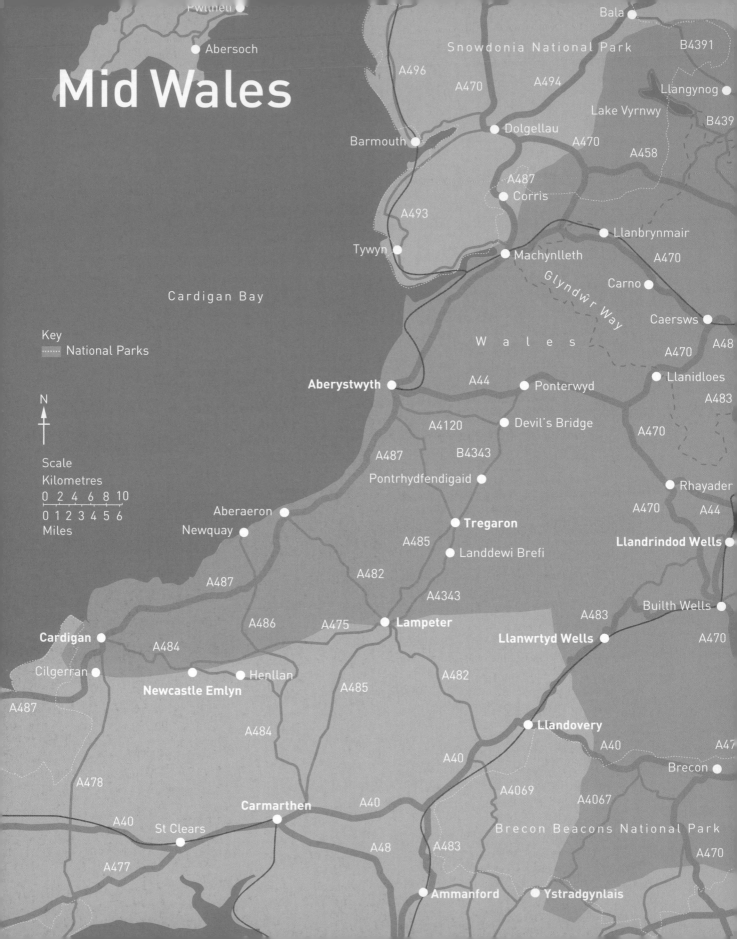

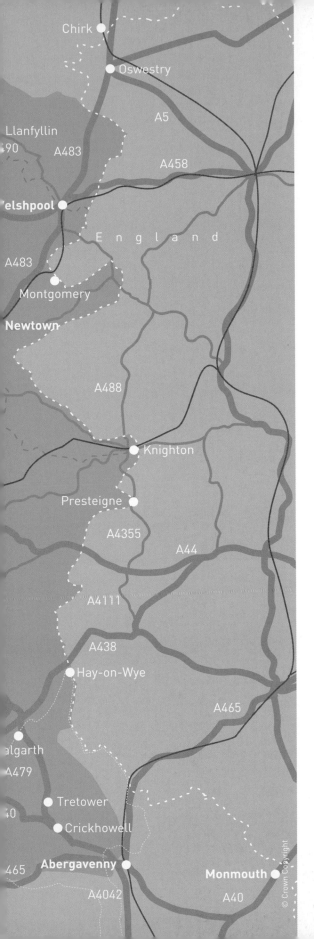

Chirk
Oswestry
A5
Llanfyllin
90
A483
A458
elshpool
E n g l a n d
A483
Montgomery
Newtown
A488
Knighton
Presteigne
A4355
A44
A4111
A438
Hay-on-Wye
A465
algarth
A479
Tretower
40
Crickhowell
465
Abergavenny
Monmouth
A4042
A40

Explore these elevated central regions of Wales with their green hills, dramatic mountains, fresh air and opportunities to relax or to be active. Visit traditional market towns, religious sites and places of industrial heritage. Go walking in the open spaces of the Brecon Beacons National Park or the Berwyn Hills. To the west is Ceredigion, with its heritage coastline and thriving centres of Welsh culture.

Mid Wales and the Brecon Beacons

Powis Castle, Presteigne Judges' Lodgings, the Glyndŵr Way, Machynlleth, Crickhowell, the Hay Literary Festival, the Brecon Jazz Festival, Dan-yr-Ogof Caves, Craig-y-Nos, Llandrindod Wells Victorian Festival, Llanwrtyd Wells bog snorkelling and Mid Wales Opera.

Above: **Waun Rydd** Walking, climbing and pot-holing are popular in the Brecon Beacons. Call at the visitor centre, near Libanus, for details of outdoor activities.

Above:
Brecon Cathedral.
As with many of Wales's ecclesiastical buildings, the marvellous interior and wonderful reverberating acoustics are put to good use for concerts as well as for services.

Above right:
Brecon Jazz Festival. The friendly atmosphere is generated as much in the streets and open spaces of the town as in the concerts given by jazz legends in concert venues.

Brecon

Among the most character-filled of Wales's market towns, Brecon's centre is a maze of narrow streets in which you will find shops – including some fine antique dealers – restaurants and ancient pubs. The town's Welsh name, Aberhonddu, estuary of the Honddu, reflects the fact that the town grew at the confluence of the rivers Honddu and Usk.
• The town centre streets are narrow and parking is scarce; use the signed car parks and enjoy exploring on foot.
www.exploremidwales.com

Brecon Cathedral. Following their conquest of Britain in 1066, the Normans quickly extended their influence into Wales. At Brecon, Benedictine monks established a priory on the site of the existing church of St John. This flourished until the dissolution of the monasteries in 1537. Almost all of Brecon Cathedral dates from this original period. The building

underwent major restoration in the 1860s under the direction of Sir Gilbert Scott. In 1923, as a result of the disestablishment of the Church in Wales in 1920, the Priory Church became the cathedral of the new diocese of Swansea and Brecon.
• There is limited parking space at the cathedral, but a walk down from the town and along the river bank is enjoyable too.
Phone: 01874 623857
www.breconcathedral.org.uk

South Wales Borderers Museum. Military regalia collections reflect the history and character of a regiment that has existed for over 300 years – with Brecon being its base for 120 of them. The gun collection traces the evolution of weapons from the 18th century to the present day. The main attraction is the Zulu War room. The exploits of the 24th Regiment during the 1879 campaign are legendary and the film "Zulu" recreated the events surrounding the heroic defence of Rorke's Drift. The compelling story is made all the more real

by the display of artefacts associated with the men who served there.
• A modest walk from the town centre, adjacent to the regimental barracks.
Phone: 01874 613310
www.rrw.org.uk

Theatr Brycheiniog. Wales is fortunate to have strong regional theatres and Theatr Brycheiniog is no exception. Since opening in 1997, it has established itself as a leading venue, presenting a diverse programme. It attracts some of the UK's top artists and companies, including The Royal National Theatre, the BBC National Orchestra of Wales, Northern Stage Ensemble, the Richard Alston Dance Company and household names in popular music, folk music and comedy. It enjoys a pleasant setting alongside the Monmouthshire and Brecon Canal.
• Event and performance details from the theatre or from the Tourist Information Centre
Phone: 01874 611622
www.theatrbrycheiniog.co.uk

Builth Wells

For four days in July, this town on the bank of the river Wye becomes a focal point for the whole nation, as visitors, exhibitors and pampered animals converge on the **Royal Welsh Agricultural Show**. This celebration of the best of country life is a great day out for all the family. There's much to see in the main ring, including the parade of winning animals each afternoon, and the myriad displays and exhibition stands are a delight. Be sure also to pop into the **Wyeside Arts Centre**, near the bridge, to see what's on there.
• Readily accessible along A-roads from all corners of Wales, as the varied accents of the farmers at the show will confirm.
www.builthwells.co.uk

Crickhowell

Delightfully situated where its fine stone-arched bridge crosses the river Usk, and surrounded by the distinctive ridged summits of the Black Mountains,

Crickhowell is a pretty town blessed with some very agreeable pubs and restaurants. It is a perfect place, in fact, for a bracing walk followed by a leisurely meal. **The Bear Hotel** which retains the atmosphere of its days as a coaching inn, is especially popular.
• Six miles westward from Abergavenny, on the A40.
Phone: 01873 810408
www.bearhotel.co.uk

Tretower Court and Castle. The stark 13th century keep of Tretower Castle stands on the remains of an earlier Norman earthwork and speaks eloquently of dangerous times. The charming manor house of Tretower Court, on the other hand, dates from the more settled 15th century, when its owners, the Vaughan family, felt secure enough to start building one of Wales's grandest medieval country residences. Open-air productions of Shakespeare are fittingly staged here each summer.
• A mile or so along the A479 from its junction with the A40 north-west of Crickhowell, marked by a vintage AA phone box.
Phone: 01874 730279
www.cadw.wales.gov.uk

Hay-on-Wye

Famous as "The Town of Books", Hay-on-Wye has more than thirty bookshops which, along with the annual literary festival, have made this previously rather sleepy border town famous around the world. The region is immortalised in the diaries of Francis Kilvert, rector of nearby Clyro, who wrote sensitively of the life of an Anglican clergyman in this corner of rural Wales during late Victorian times.
• Right on the border with England, on the A438 north-east of Brecon.
www.exploremidwales.com

Knighton

This attractive town is home to an interactive exhibition describing the history, flora and fauna of Offa's Dyke, the

Left:
The Glyndŵr Way. One of numerous well-signed routes passing through historic regions of Wales.

Below:
Llanidloes. The timbered buildings of the town square and China Street lend a quaint dignity to the attractive centre of Llanidloes.

Right:
Monmouthshire and Brecon Canal. Originally built to serve industry, many of Wales's historic canals and railways may be enjoyed under more leisurely circumstances today.

earthwork that has more or less marked the border between Wales and England since Saxon times. The Offa's Dyke Path national trail extends 177 miles (285km) from the mouth of the Wye at Sedbury, near Chepstow, northward to Prestatyn in Flintshire, with Knighton at about the halfway point.
• On the A488, some eighteen miles north-east of Llandrindod Wells.
www.exploremidwales.com

Glyndŵr Way National Trail. This 132-mile route links many locations associated with Owain Glyndŵr's campaigns for Welsh independence. From Sycharth near Welshpool, where the hospitality of his court was legendary, to the borderlands around Knighton, the path passes through areas where he fought many battles and generated unshakeable loyalty.
• Obtain detailed maps and guidebooks from Tourist Information Centres and local bookshops.

Llanidloes

Four streets meet at the black-and-white timbered market hall, built on wooden stilts, in this attractive town centre. An exhibition about timber-framed buildings is open throughout the year. The museum of local history tells the story of agriculture, mining, and the rise of nonconformism and Chartism in the region.
• South-west of Newtown, on the main A470 road that runs the length of Wales.
www.llanidloes.com

Minerva Arts Centre. The woollen industry, which was important to the economy of this region for centuries, has a shop window at the Minerva Arts Centre. Here, at the home of the Quilt Association, you will discover displays of antique quilts, including styles produced in Wales over the past two centuries, as well as the frames, templates and other equipment with which they were made. The centre also hosts workshops,

lectures and courses.
• In the centre of Llanidloes.
Phone: 01686 413467
www.quilt.org.uk

Llanwrtyd Wells

Let's just say that here, in a place that describes itself as "The Wackiest Town in Britain", you are likely to encounter some pretty unusual goings-on. We're not talking ancient traditions here. It was the local pub landlord, Gordon Green MBE, who enriched the world by devising the sport of **bog-snorkelling**, along with a series of other distinctive events. These include the **Man versus Horse Marathon**, **the Morris in the Forest folk dancing festival**, and the **Real Ale Wobble**, a two day mountain-biking and beer drinking festival.
• Between Builth Wells and Llandovery, on the A483.
www.exploremidwales.com

Machynlleth

Machynlleth occupies a special place in Welsh history, as centre of the revolution by which Owain Glyndŵr reasserted Welsh identity at the beginning of the 15th century. The building believed to have been used for his parliament of 1404 still stands. The busy main street has attractive shops and pubs, overlooked by an impressive Gothic Revival clocktower. The Tabernacle, a former Wesleyan chapel, houses the **Museum of Modern Art Wales,** with its excellent auditorium, recording studio, exhibition spaces, artists' studios and rehearsal rooms. It is the main venue for the **Machynlleth Festival** which is held in late August.
• From the clocktower, **The Tabernacle** is a short walk along the road towards Dolgellau, and the parliament building is along the main street, on the left.
Phone: 01654 703355 (The Tabernacle)
www.momawales.org.uk

Museum of Mechanical Magic, Llanbrynmair. This collection of moving figures, mechanical toys and automata, all of which display superb craftsmanship, will amuse and entertain visitors of all ages. Open all year, it also features a giant moving dragon, a rabbit village, the Timberkits factory, a shop and a café.
• Between Machynlleth and Caersws, on the A470.
Phone: 01650 511514

Montgomery

This beautifully picturesque border town is set around a central square, where the petite town hall and the distinguished architecture of the houses make you feel as if you are on the set of a historical drama.
• South of Welshpool along B-roads from Garthmyl or Kingswood.
www.exploremidwales.com

Newtown

Occupying a strategic position at a bridging point on the river Severn, Newtown is a busy centre of local government and commerce. Highlights include **the Robert Owen** and **WH Smith museums, Theatr Hafren,** the contemporary **Oriel Davies Gallery** and the **Textile Museum,** which celebrates the region's woollen and flannel industry. The world's first mail-order shopping service – Pryce-Jones, which listed Queen Victoria amongst its customers – operated from the large red-brick warehouse that still overlooks the town.
• There's a large car park off the A489.
www.exploremidwales.com

Mid Wales Opera. Founded in 1988, the award-winning Mid Wales Opera has established itself as one of the UK's foremost touring opera companies. Its productions have been performed in over eighty venues in the UK and Ireland. From the elegant Opera House at Buxton, and Aldeburgh's Snape Maltings, to the intimate theatre at Felin-Fach, Lampeter, the company's annual visit is eagerly anticipated by opera lovers throughout the country.
• You will find the programme in local

Far right:
Montgomery Castle. The hilltop site of Montgomery Castle was chosen for its defensive advantages, including the wide views over the surrounding countryside, which may be enjoyed under more peaceful circumstances today.

Right:
Museum of Modern Art Wales. This ceramic head was sculpted by Mihangel Arfor Jones and is one of many pieces on display at the Museum of Modern Art Wales.

Below:
Bog-snorkelling. If you can find the motivation to submerge yourself in the cold brown waters of the bog-snorkelling course at Llanwrtyd Wells, and power your way to the finish in a winning time, you will have a great story to tell for many years to come!

Left:
Powis Castle. This statue of a shepherd merrily playing a flute looks out over the fine gardens of Powis Castle.

Below:
Dan-yr-Ogof Caves. The underground tour of the Dan-yr-Ogof Caves is memorable; the occasional concerts held there equally so.

papers, from Tourist Information Centres and via a link from the Arts Council of Wales website.
Phone: 01938 500611
www.midwalesopera.co.uk

Presteigne

This fascinating little town sits on the border between Wales and Herefordshire. Its half-timbered buildings date from the 14th century. Enter the fascinating world of Victorian judges, their servants and their felonious guests as you explore the cells, courtroom and living quarters of the **Judges' Lodgings**, the town's award-winning, hands-on family museum.
• Travel eastward from Llandrindod Wells on the A44 and B4362.
Phone: 01544 260650 (TIC)
www.judgeslodging.org.uk

Upper Tawe Valley

Dan-yr-Ogof Caves. The emergence of the River Llynfell from a cave was a mystery to local people until, in 1912, Tommy and Jeff Morgan found the courage to explore further. Using only candles to light their way, and arrows in the sand to find their way back, they discovered a wonderland of stalactites and stalagmites. When they found an underground lake, deep inside the mountain, they returned with coracles and sculled across not just one lake, but four. Since then cavers have found over ten miles (16km) of amazing caves. The journey through the illuminated Dan-yr-Ogof Caves is an experience you will never forget. On the surface, the Shire Horse Centre, farm, museum and life-sized dinosaurs will make your visit complete.
• From J43 on the M4, the A465 north-eastward to the A4221 and A4067 combines speed and scenery.
Phone: 01639 730284
www.showcaves.co.uk

Craig-y-Nos. This early Victorian country house in the upper Swansea Valley was bought in 1878 by the opera singer Adelina

Patti, who could fairly be described as an international superstar of her day. She created a stylish retreat where she could recharge her energy between tours.
This was one of the first private homes in Britain to have electricity, which enabled Adelina to install the latest lighting technology in her theatre. An electric Orchestrion organ – driven by that early form of digital music, punched paper rolls – was also acquired. Following dedicated fundraising and restoration efforts, Craig-y-Nos is now a hotel, and the beautiful theatre hosts regular recitals and concerts.
• Near the Dan-yr-Ogof Caves on the A4067.
Phone: 01639 730205
www.craigynoscastle.co.uk

Welshpool

This bustling market town serves a large agricultural hinterland and has the largest sheep market in Europe. It is a pleasant walk from the town centre to Powis Castle, through parkland designed by Capability Brown. Or stroll along the towpath of the **Montgomery Canal** to the **Powysland Museum**, where you will learn about the Stone Age inhabitants, Roman settlement, Viking attacks and the growth of Christianity in the area. Allow plenty of time to explore both Powis Castle and the town, with its broad main thoroughfare.
• www.exploremidwales.com

Powis Castle. Originally a fortress of the Welsh Princes of Powys, and built around 1200, this sumptuous castle was remodelled over four centuries by the Herbert family. Its outstandingly fine gardens – laid out in French and Italian styles and overhung with enormous clipped yew trees – shelter rare and tender plants, including grapevines. The castle contains historically important furniture and paintings. Treasures from India are displayed in the **Clive Museum** – Edward, son of Robert Clive of India, married Lady Henrietta Herbert in 1784.
• Prominently signed from the A458 and A483 south-west of Welshpool.

Phone: 01938 551929
www.nationaltrust.org.uk

Welshpool and Llanfair Light Railway.
One of Wales's "Great Little Railways", this
narrow-gauge steam railway runs between
Welshpool and Llanfair Caereinion, through
the glorious countryside of the Banwy valley.
• Llanfair Caereinion is nine miles west of
Welshpool, on the A458.
Phone: 01938 810441
www.wllr.org.uk

Sculpture Trail at Lake Vyrnwy. Each
summer for several years beginning in
1999, sculptors from countries all over
northern Europe, including Scandinavia,
the Baltic States and Russia, gathered at
Lake Vyrnwy for an international
symposium. The results of their efforts
form the Lake Vyrnwy Sculpture Trail,
spectacularly positioned below the dam of
this enormous reservoir, which has more
than sixty works skilfully shaped from local
pine. These fill the available space at Lake
Vyrnwy but the tradition continues in new
locations around mid Wales.
• The B4393 from Llanfyllin meanders
around the far end of the lake and back.
Phone: 01691 870278
www.waterscape.com

Festivals and events

Hay Festival of Literature. Near the end of
May each year, the population of this small
border town increases dramatically as
famous authors and celebrities, and
thousands of devoted readers of their
books, gather for this annual banquet of
literary delights. The prodigious events
programme includes talks and interviews
in the festival's marquees, followed by
signings in the on-site bookshop and an
impressive choice of spoken, dramatic and
musical entertainment each evening.
• The good humour of staff manning
temporary car parks eases your arrival and
sets the tone for an enjoyable day.
Phone: 0870 990 1299
www.hayfestival.com

Brecon Jazz Festival. There's something
about jazz, especially when played in the
open air, that lifts the spirits. Every **August**,
top performers in all styles of jazz bring
their sounds to the main square, market
hall, car parks, **Theatr Brycheiniog** and
hotels of Brecon, for one of the UK's best
jazz festivals.
• Be prepared to park some distance away
and to be on your feet – spectating or
dancing – as the music exerts its magic.
Phone: 01874 625511
www.breconjazz.co.uk

Llandrindod Wells. Towards the end of
August, the dignified streets and handsome
gardens of Llandrindod Wells celebrate the
town's origins as a 19th century spa resort.
Residents and visitors alike dress up to
enjoy themed events, including street
theatre, music-hall performances and
traditional sports and games. Don't miss
the funfair, food and craft stalls and the
elegant **Pump Rooms** – where you may
partake of afternoon tea to the
accompaniment of congenial music.
• On the A483 north of Builth Wells, with
broad streets and ample parking.
www.llandrindod.co.uk

Presteigne Music Festival. Founded in
1983, this annual gathering has a
reputation for excellence. It attracts
performers and composers of distinction
and has received glowing endorsements in
the music media, including BBC Radio 3.
It organises workshop sessions in local
schools, at which professional musicians
inspire children with performances of
classical music, and it is especially known
for nurturing talented performers early in
their careers.
• The regional music festivals of Wales are
served by links from the Arts Council of
Wales website.
Phone: 01544 267800
www.presteignefestival.com

Right:
**Llandrindod Wells
Victorian Festival.**
"Queen Victoria"
and her entourage
go on stately
walkabout through
the crowds at this
popular festival.

Below:
Lake Vyrnwy. The
Sculpture Trail at
Lake Vyrnwy is a
visual and tactile
delight – huge
blocks of timber
have been carved
and assembled in
ways that will
stimulate and
provoke.

Ceredigion

Aberystwyth, Llywernog silver and lead mine museum, Strata Florida Abbey, Lampeter, the Vale of Rheidol Railway, Llanerchaeron, Cardigan, the Aberystwyth Arts Centre, the National Library of Wales and the Tregaron Welsh Gold Centre.

Above:
National Library of Wales, Aberystwyth. The Library includes many rare books including the first book printed in Welsh in 1546 and the first Welsh translation of the complete Bible in 1588. It also has the earliest surviving manuscript entirely in Welsh known as 'The Black Book of Carmarthen'.

Above:
The Harbourmaster. Hotel. Occupies the building from which the harbourmaster once trained his telescope on ships sailing in.

Aberaeron

Once a small fishing village, Aberaeron grew (following the creation of its harbour between 1807 and 1811) into one of the major trading and shipbuilding ports of Cardigan Bay. With the expansion of the harbour came the expansion of local enterprise; the site of the local woollen mill still stands and the ironworks produced the famous Aberaeron shovel. Today the town is still a focal point for local communities but the main industry is now tourism.

The Harbourmaster Hotel at Aberaeron, where the eponymous official once trained his telescope on ships sailing in, has stylishly contemporary interiors and an imaginative menu based on fine local produce such as Cardigan Bay crab and lobster, and Aberaeron mackerel. The Harbourmaster is a Grade II listed building, dating back to 1811.
Phone: 01545 570755
www.harbour-master.com

Aberystwyth

The university town of **Aberystwyth** grew from a small settlement guarded by one of the first of Edward I's castles, built in 1277, which stands ruined on its breezy promontory overlooking the bay. Inland, Llanbadarn Fawr, its church austerely spiritual in the Celtic fashion, is where the 6th century scholar-saint Padarn founded his monastery. During the 19th century, the harbour handled lead and zinc from mines in the hills, and general cargo from around the Irish Sea. With the arrival of the railway in 1864, the town became a popular seaside resort. The wide promenade and the railway to the top of Constitution Hill still attract the crowds.
• The A470 and A44, from the direction of Newtown, take you across the bare terrain of the Cambrian mountains.
www.aberystwyth-online.co.uk

Far left:
Ceredigion Museum. Western Wales is the last place in Britain were the coracle remains in use. It is often thought of as uniquely Welsh but similar craft evolved in Scotland, Ireland and elsewhere around the world.

Left:
Aberystwyth's Constitution Hill. The summit offers tremendous views over Aberystwyth and across Cardigan Bay to the Llŷn Peninsula and Pembrokeshire.

Below:
Aberystwyth Arts Centre. National Youth Theatre of Wales production of Whisper in the Woods.

National Library of Wales. Overlooking the town from its commanding hilltop site, Aberystwyth's eyrie of erudition is one of the great libraries of the world. Since 1911, it has enjoyed the right to acquire a free copy of every printed work published in Britain and Ireland. It holds a huge collection of works about Wales and the other Celtic countries, in the form of books and pamphlets, magazines and newspapers, microforms, ephemera and a wealth of digital material. Thousands of manuscripts and archives, pictures and photographs, maps, sound recordings and moving images are available for research, and there are many treasures on public display. 'The Drwm', a multi-media auditorium, brings the library's rich collections to life in new ways that enthuse and involve its visitors. The varied program includes musical and theatrical performances, book launches, lectures and world-class films. The library also arranges exhibitions throughout the year.
• There is parking near the library, which can be seen for miles around, and there are regular buses up the steep hill to the university campus.
Phone: 01970 632800
www.llgc.org.uk

Aberystwyth Arts Centre. The award-winning Aberystwyth Arts Centre is among the largest and busiest in Wales, with a wide-ranging programme of events and activities across all art forms. It welcomes over 500,000 visitors a year, including over 70,000 participants in its community arts and education programme. It is a department of the University of Wales, Aberystwyth, and sits at the heart of the university campus.
• As part of the spacious campus, access and parking are straightforward.
Phone: 01970 623232
www.aberystwythartscentre.co.uk

Vale of Rheidol Railway. The gleaming steam trains of this preserved narrow-gauge railway huff and puff their way up the twisting valley of the river Rheidol from Aberystwyth's main station to picturesque **Pontarfynach**, or **Devil's Bridge**. The hugely appealing scenery belies the industrial purpose of the line, which opened in 1902 to serve the nearby lead mines, though passengers and timber also became mainstays of its traffic.
• Enjoyable signposted walks radiate from the vicinity of the falls.
Phone: 01970 625819
www.rheidolrailway.co.uk

Ceredigion Museum. This informative museum is attractively housed in the former Coliseum theatre and cinema. Its displays cover the rich history of this fascinating and largely rural region of Wales: they highlight the significance of agriculture, seafaring and lead mining. There is also a gallery displaying a changing programme of visual art.
• There is usually parking space along the promenade, giving a good excuse to explore the nearby town centre on foot.
Phone: 01970 633088
www.ceredigion.gov.uk

Constitution Hill. For spectacular views over Cardigan Bay and much of Ceredigion, take the cliff railway to the 430-foot (131m) summit of Aberystwyth's Constitution Hill, at the northern end of the promenade. Originally operated by means of a water-balanced funicular system, the railway was equipped with electric winding equipment in 1921. The Camera Obscura projects images of the bay, the town and the surrounding countryside onto a large white table; it opened in 1985 as a reconstruction of a popular Victorian attraction.
• The lower station is located just behind the terraced boarding houses and hotels of the promenade.
www.aberystwyth-online.co.uk

Aeron Valley

Llanerchaeron. Set in beautiful Dyffryn Aeron, the Aeron valley, this fine house has altered little since it was designed by

John Nash in the 1790s. It is the most complete example of his early work. This was a self-sufficient estate, with home farm, dairy, laundry, brewery and salting house. Today it is a working organic farm, producing home-grown produce.
• Two miles inland from Aberaeron, on the A482.
Phone: 01545 570200
www.nationaltrust.org.uk

....

Cardigan

Cardigan – Aberteifi. It was here in 1176, in the castle overlooking the river, that Lord Rhys ap Gruffudd – premier among regional Welsh rulers at the time – held what is regarded as the first national eisteddfod. The tradition grew whereby the best poets and musicians of the day were rewarded by being invited to a chair at the top table, an honour echoed in today's eisteddfod chairing ceremony. At nearby St Dogmael's, the church contains the 6th century Sagranus stone which – by commemorating the Irish ruler buried there in both Latin and the ancient Ogham script – made possible the deciphering of the early Irish language. Cardigan is an important place of pilgrimage for the Roman Catholic church; the national shrine of Wales is at the church of Our Lady of the Taper.
• This important regional centre has a thriving high street, which fills with stalls for the traditional fair each November.
www.visitcardigan.com

Cardigan Heritage Centre. Visit this 18th century warehouse on the bank of the river Teifi to learn all about the history of Cardigan. The town has many places of historical interest including the **castle**, **priory**, **Shire Hall**, **Guildhall** and several **churches**. One of the Russian guns faced by the Light Brigade of the 11th Hussars as they made their disastrous charge at Balaclava during the Crimean War, under the command of the Earl of Cardigan, stands outside the Guildhall.
• Local guidebooks and leaflets are

available from the Tourist Information Centre and the excellent local shops.
Phone: 01239 614404
www.ceredigion.gov.uk

Theatr Mwldan. Established in 1983 by Cardigan Theatre, a local amateur company, this thriving theatre has grown, following a £7 million development project, into a multi-purpose centre for the arts. It has two theatres, a rehearsal studio and a visual arts exhibition space, along with excellent front-of-house and dining amenities. More than five thousand people pass through its doors each week.
• Call in for a programme and inspect whatever is on in the exhibition gallery.
Phone: 01239 621200
www.mwldan.co.uk

....

Lampeter

Lampeter is home to the oldest college of the University of Wales: its specialisation in religious studies and the liberal arts dates back to 1822. To the north-east, on the scenic B4343 towards Tregaron, is **Llanddewi Brefi** where you will find a church dedicated to David, the patron saint of Wales. It was here that the ground is said to have risen beneath his feet, so that he could be better seen and heard by his eager congregation.
• Some twenty-eight miles south of Aberystwyth, along the A485.
www.tourism.ceredigion.gov.uk

Theatr Felinfach. Many visiting companies are amazed to see a fully equipped theatre here in the far west of Wales, and to see it brimming with life. They quickly realise that the theatre's strength derives from its solid foundations in the region's vibrant Welsh-language culture, and that it belongs to people of all age groups and backgrounds.
• At Felinfach in the Aeron valley (A482) between Lampeter and Aberaeron.
Phone: 01570 470697
www.ceredigion.gov.uk

Teifi Valley Railway. Created from a branch of the Great Western Railway, this short but scenic line offers splendid views of the beautiful Teifi valley and a nostalgic reminder of the days of steam. With unspoilt woodland to either side, the train passes ancient stone workings along the route of an ancient drovers' trail as it follows the bank of the Teifi. You may disembark and watch the crew as they uncouple the engine and move it to the front of the train for your return journey. Back in the station yard at Henllan, you can get a refreshing cup of tea and a sandwich in the tea room.
• Henllan is a couple of miles east of Newcastle Emlyn, on the A484.
Phone: 01559 371077
www. teifivalleyrailway.com

New Quay

With its picturesque houses, pubs and restaurants clinging to the hills above the blue waters of Cardigan Bay, this small port and seaside resort has great character. During its 19th century heyday as a shipbuilding centre, some 250 sailing vessels – sloops, smacks, ketches and schooners – were launched here.
• From the A487 at Synod Inn, between Cardigan and Aberaeron, take the A486.
www.tourism.ceredigion.gov.uk

Ponterwyd

Llywernog Silver and Lead Mine Museum. Head inland from Aberystwyth and you will soon find yourself enjoying remarkable vistas of stark moorland above snug green valleys. The Automobile Association has described the B4574 through Cwm Ystwyth as one of the ten most scenic drives in the world. Hereabouts, in conditions that make you marvel at their toughness, people once mined a range of metal ores, including rock containing the precious silver that was made into coins at a Royal Mint in Aberystwyth.
• The Llywernog Mining Museum is off the A44 near Ponterwyd.

Phone: 01970 890620
www.silverminetours.co.uk

Tregaron

The Welsh Gold Centre and Gallery. On the square in Tregaron, you will find a fine statue of **Henry Richard MP** – local chapel stalwart, secretary of the Peace Society and early advocate of a League of Nations. Nearby is The Welsh Gold Centre, the premises of Rhiannon Jewellery, where you may watch the jeweller and her staff working gold and silver into intricate designs, many of them inspired by Celtic art and legend. Work by artists in a range of materials is shown in the centre's gallery and shop.
• On the A485, eleven miles north-east of Lampeter, eighteen miles south-east of Aberystwyth.
Phone: 01974 298415
www.rhiannon.co.uk

Strata Florida Abbey. Standing serenely in its remote valley, the 12th century Cistercian abbey of Strata Florida – Vale of Flowers – was an important religious house and an influential centre of Welsh culture, patronised by princes and poets. Dafydd ap Gwilym, the greatest of Welsh medieval poets, is commemorated here. The Romanesque west doorway, the abbey's most striking feature, frames the hills where the monks once farmed. The south transept features fine medieval floor tiles.
• Turn off the B4343 at Pontrhydfendigaid, five miles north-east of Tregaron.
Phone: 01974 831261
www.cadw.wales.co.uk

Festivals and events

Aberystwyth MusicFest. A glittering line-up of celebrated artists leads a programme of the highest quality music-making and teaching at Aberystwyth's International Festival and Summer School each **July**. The shared enjoyment of audience, student and artist creates a refreshing and

Top left:
Strata Florida. A monastic community founded in 1164.

Above:
Aberystwyth and Ceredigion County Show. One of the many equestrian events at the Show.

Far left:
Cardigan Bay Seafood Festival. Held in mid **July** when the local catch is plentiful.

Left:
Aberystwyth Farmers' Market . Open air stalls sell a wide range of fresh, local produce.

inspirational community atmosphere.
• The websites of the Arts Council of Wales and Cerdd Ystwyth (Aberystwyth's music shop) carry authoritative programmes. www.aberystwythartscentre.co.uk/musicfest

Cardigan River and Food Festival. An annual event that celebrates the River Teifi and the diversity of food grown and prepared in the area. A one-day event, held in mid **August**, the festival boasts a variety of food stalls, cooking demonstrations, river activities and boat races.
• Contact: Matthew Newbold
Phone: 01239 615554
www.visitcardigan.com/cardigan-festivals-river-food.shtm

Cardigan Bay Seafood Festival. Held on the quaysides around Aberaeron's picturesque harbour each **July**, this is where to sample mouth-watering local fish and shellfish. There are mackerel barbecues, crab-picking and catching competitions, whelk racing, brass bands,

jazz, shanty singers and beach art.
• Contact: Harbourmaster Hotel
Phone: 01545 570755

Aberystwyth and Ceredigion County Show. Held at the Gelli Angharad fields every **June**, this enjoyable agricultural show attracts visitors from all over Ceredigion and beyond. The main elements are the livestock competitions (including categories for horses, cattle and poultry) and the popular dog shows.
Phone: 01974 298 367
www.aberystwythshow.com

Aberystwyth Farmers' Market. This is one of the largest farmers' markets Wales, hosting up to 30 stalls on the first and third Saturdays each month, at Aberystwyth's North Parade. There is a wide range of produce (including organic), plants and craft items.
Phone: 01970 633066

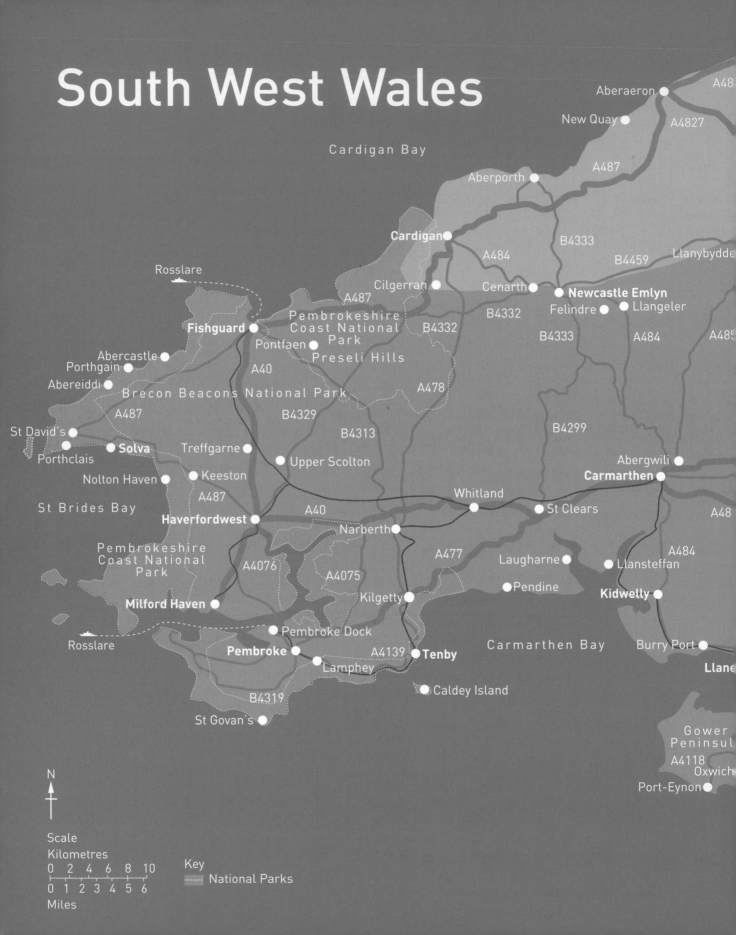

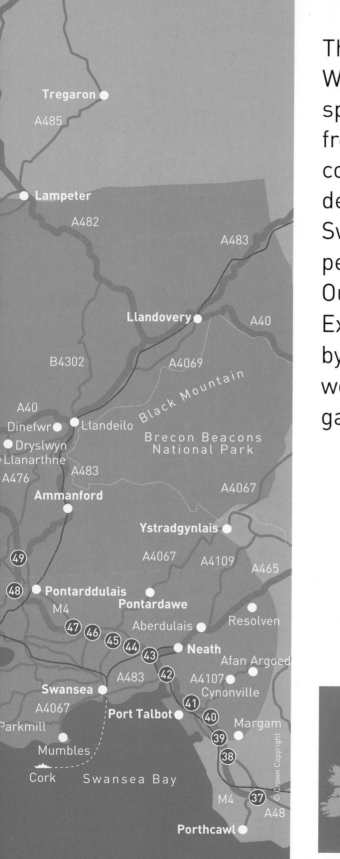

Tregaron

A485

Lampeter

A482

A483

Llandovery

A40

B4302

A4069

A40

Black Mountain

Dinefwr

Llandeilo

Dryslwyn

Brecon Beacons
National Park

Llanarthne

A483

A476

A4067

Ammanford

Ystradgynlais

A4067

A4109

A465

49

48

Pontarddulais

Pontardawe

M4

Aberdulais

Resolven

47 46

45 44

43

Neath

Afan Argoed

A483

42

A4107

Cynonville

Swansea

41

A4067

Port Talbot

Margam

Parkmill

40

Mumbles

39

38

Cork

Swansea Bay

M4

37

A48

Porthcawl

© Crown Copyright

The south-western region of Wales is bounded by a spectacular coastline extending from Pembrokeshire (the only coast in England and Wales to be designated a national park) to Swansea Bay. The Gower peninsula is an Area of Outstanding Natural Beauty. Explore Swansea, Wales's "city by the sea", and discover the wonderful countryside and gardens of Carmarthenshire.

Pembrokeshire

Ancient monuments and historic harbours abound in this long-populated region. Explore St David's Cathedral, the Landsker line, Milford Haven, Haverfordwest, Solva, Tenby, the Preseli Hills, Pentre Ifan, Caldey Island and Castell Henllys.

Above:
Pembroke Castle. The intimidating central tower, and the natural moat provided by the estuary, would have made any attacker think twice.

Above:
Caldey Abbey.
The monks of
Caldey Island
combine a spiritual
lifestyle with sound
business acumen as
they promote their
popular products
locally, by mail
order and on the
internet.

Above right:
Ceibwr area.
Some six miles
(9km) from its
northern end, the
Pembrokeshire
Coast Path passes
the small port of
Ceibwr and follows
high cliffs above
caves and a natural
arch.

Castles. Pembrokeshire is dotted with many castles, large and small. The powerful keep of the imposing castle in **Pembroke** speaks of the bitter conflict between the Welsh and the Normans. Delightful **Carew**, with its tidal mill, illustrates the transition from stronghold to country house; one of the finest Celtic crosses in Wales stands nearby. **Manorbier** was the birthplace of traveller and scholar-cleric Gerald of Wales. **Picton Castle** has been in the hands of the same family since the 15th century and houses fine furniture and an art gallery. But it was the series of small castles along the **Landsker line**, between **Llawhaden** and **St David's**, that defined the character of the county. The region to the south of the line, including the ports of **Milford Haven** and **Tenby**, was occupied in medieval times by English settlers and their Flemish allies and came to be known as "the little England beyond Wales".

• www.visitpembrokeshire.com

The Pembrokeshire Coast Path.
A 179-mile (288km) national trail around the south-western peninsula of Wales – the only stretch of coastline in England and Wales to be designated a National Park. As well as being outstandingly scenic, this coast abounds in prehistoric monuments, industrial heritage sites and fascinating seaports. The path passes close to Tenby, Pembroke, Milford Haven, Solva, St David's and Fishguard.

• The path links St Dogmael's, near Cardigan, and Amroth in the south of the county – the official National Trail Guide is widely available from bookshops and tourist information centres.

Caldey Island

A pleasant boat trip from Tenby will take you to Caldey Island, where you may explore the **Old Priory** and the medieval churches of **St David** and **St Illtyd**, and are welcome to join the monks at one of their chanted services in the Abbey Church.

Caldey Abbey was originally built in 1910 by Anglican Benedictine monks, though it later became a Cistercian community. It was designed in Italianate style by Penarth-based architect John Coates-Carter and is now a listed building. The monks are famous for making perfumes, chocolate and shortbread, which are sold in the village. **The Post Office** is also a museum giving an insight into the island's history. There are also some marvellous walks on the island.
• There are regular boat services from Tenby during the holiday season.
Phone: 01834 844453
www.caldey-island.co.uk

Cardigan

Cilgerran Castle. The time-worn towers of Cilgerran rise majestically above woodland on the rim of the deep Teifi gorge. Originally one of the strongholds of the Welsh region of Deheubarth, it was extended by the Norman baron William Marshall. He added the powerful towers and thick curtain wall that so inspired JMW Turner and the many Victorian travellers who came upriver by boat from Cardigan to savour its romance.
• South of Cardigan, off the A478.
Phone: 01239 621339
www.cadw.wales.gov.uk

Castell Henllys reconstructed Iron Age settlement. This scheduled ancient monument is an Iron Age hill fort dating from around 600 BC. A great deal of information about its origins has been discovered by archaeologists and you can learn all about their current excavations. Thatched buildings have been reconstructed on their original foundations: the chieftain's house, the granary and the smithy may all be seen in authentic guise. A sculpture trail depicts Celtic myths and legends, and there is a farm with ancient breeds of livestock.
• Near Eglwyswrw, on the A487 south-west of Cardigan.
Phone: 01239 891319
www.castellhenllys.com

Fishguard

Long established as a ferry port for Ireland, Fishguard combines a bustling town centre with the peace and quiet of the Lower Harbour, with its old stone quay and picturesque buildings. It was just along the coast, at **Carregwastad Point**, that the last invasion force to land in Britain came ashore in 1797.

A rag-tag army of around a thousand untrained French troops, mostly convicts released for the task, led by the disaffected Irish-American William Tate, attempted to raise support for a French invasion of Ireland. They were met by the sight of lines of people along the cliff-tops, including women in traditional red shawls and tall hats, who gave a good impression of a large garrison of soldiers. By the time the actual militia arrived, the French had been persuaded of the folly of their mission by, amongst others, the formidable blacksmith and cobbler Jemima Nicholas and her pitchfork. The story is told at the **Royal Oak pub**, where the surrender was accepted.
• The A40 and A487 converge on Fishguard, but consider also the scenic approach along the B4313.
www.abergwaun.com

Melin Tregwynt Woollen Mill. This beautiful whitewashed mill, owned by the same family since 1912, is located in a remote wooded valley off the A487 between Fishguard and St David's. As far back as the 17th century, local farmers used to bring their fleeces here to be spun into yarn and woven into blankets for their families. The mill continues to use traditional methods to produce blankets, spreads and throws of the highest quality, but with a fresh approach to design and colour. You can watch the weaving on weekdays throughout the year and the shop sells a wide selection of Melin Tregwynt products.
• Signed down minor roads to the coast, some four miles south-west of Fishguard.
Phone: 01348 891644
www.melintregwynt.co.uk

Right:
Cilgerran Castle. With its stout defences and elevated position, Cilgerran Castle enabled its occupants to dominate the Teifi valley.

Below:
Castell Henllys. The reconstructed Iron Age settlement at Castell Henllys is based on detailed archaeological investigation and portrays both the comforts and the dangers of daily life there.

Below right:
Royal Oak pub. Pop into the Royal Oak pub in Fishguard to learn all about the last time an invasion force landed on the British mainland.

LAST INVASION OF
BRITAIN PEACE TREATY
WAS SIGNED HERE
IN 1797

Haverfordwest

Remarkably, for somewhere so far from the sea, Haverfordwest grew as a port to serve the Norman castle and the town that grew around it from the 12th century onwards. But it was the Flemish immigrants into southern Pembrokeshire who, a couple of centuries later, developed the town into an important centre for wool, leather, dairy produce and brewing, and who exported the fruits of their energetic labour from the river quayside. The upper reaches of the Cleddau estuary had several small ports – Landshipping and Lawrenny amongst them – from which the hard coal mined in the area was transported.
• The town is easily accessible via the A40.

Haverfordwest Town Museum. The history of the castle and town of Haverfordwest, county town of Pembrokeshire for almost a thousand years, is on display here, illuminated by intriguing exhibits and a multimedia presentation. The museum is adjacent to the early-12th century castle, which dominates the skyline of the town. Only the shell remains, but the old prison and police station inside the walls house the county archives.
• There is parking space around the town, which is a good place to explore on foot.
Phone: 01437 763087
www.haverfordwest-town-museum.org.uk

Nant y Coy Mill, Treffgarne Gorge. This restored 14th century corn mill sits in a picturesque setting below **Great Treffgarne rocks**, near Haverfordwest. A nature trail runs alongside the stream that powers the mill. You will also find a small museum, a craft shop and a tea room.
• Five miles north of Haverfordwest, on the A40 towards Fishguard.
Phone: 01437 741671

Nolton Haven. The attractive village of Nolton Haven is typical of the many places in Pembrokeshire where you will find plenty to do. It has a popular riding centre and a quaint schoolroom, which is the venue for art exhibitions during the summer months. Traditional Welsh food and entertainment enliven the audiences at Celtic Corner.
• Take the A487 from Haverfordwest to Simpson Cross, then narrow lanes to the village.

Pembrokeshire Motor Museum. At Keeston Hill, near Haverfordwest, you will find on display an interesting range of locally owned veteran, vintage and classic cars, motorcycles and bikes. There is often work going on in the restoration workshop and the staff will be pleased to explain the intricacies of the fine vehicles in their care.
• About three miles north-west of Haverfordwest, on the A487 towards St David's.
Phone: 01437 710950
www.pembrokeshiremotormuseum.co.uk

Scolton Manor House and Country Park. You gain a strong impression of the daily life of the occupants of this Victorian manor from its "upstairs, downstairs" exhibits and historical artefacts. The surrounding country park has an ecological theme and hosts numerous events in the summer: its attractions include a steam train, smithy and wheelwright's workshop.
• Four miles north-east of Haverfordwest, on the B4329 towards Cardigan.
Phone: 01437 731328
www.pembrokeshire.gov.uk

Milford Haven

The **Cleddau estuary** is a remarkable geographical feature: a ria, or submerged river valley, providing superb shelter for ships. Nelson declared it one of the best natural harbours he had seen anywhere in the world. Once infamous as a hideaway for pirates and smugglers, Milford saw several failed attempts at reinvention – as a naval dockyard, a transatlantic passenger port and (with temporary success) as a fishing harbour. Today, the Milford Haven Waterway is a thriving centre for aquatic

sports, with several marinas and sailing schools. It is also one of the UK's main ports for the import of oil.
• The A477 from Pembroke takes you high over the Cleddau estuary. It is worth a detour.

Milford Haven Museum. Housed in a former warehouse on the quayside at Milford Marina, this museum was once a working part of its subject matter. It re-creates Milford Haven's colourful past, focusing, naturally, on the maritime history of the town and the Cleddau waterway.
• The drive down to the harbour reveals the snug shelter provided within its walls.
Phone: 01646 694496

Upton Castle Gardens. These delightful gardens encompass 35 acres of parkland with a wide variety of trees and shrubs on thickly wooded slopes overlooking the waters of Milford Haven. Particularly noted for its rhododendrons, camellias and magnolias, there are also formal terraces with herbaceous borders, rose gardens and over 250 species of trees and shrubs. There is also a medieval chapel within the grounds.
• Phone: 01646 651782

Pembroke

The attractive main street of Pembroke, with the intimidating mass of the castle at one end, has attractive Georgian architecture, shops and pubs. **Pembroke Dock** is where a largely imported and notoriously unruly workforce constructed 269 wooden-hulled vessels for the Royal Navy between 1814 and 1926. The naval dockyard was overtaken by developments in technology as iron and steel construction became universal. The functional architecture of the buildings has a distinctive charm: there is nothing quite like them anywhere else in Wales.
• Pembroke's castle entrance and main street are a rather steep climb from the quayside car park.
www.pembroke-dock.co.uk

Pembroke Dock Gun Tower. This Martello tower was built to protect the naval dockyard, a vital strategic asset and a likely target for attack. It is equipped as it would have looked when it was in use around the end of the 19th century – complete with cannon and defending soldiers.
• There are quiet corners among the stout buildings where the present day recedes and the past speaks eloquently.
Phone: 01646 622246
www.pembroke-dock.co.uk

Lamphey Bishop's Palace. Near Pembroke, the bishops of St David's built themselves a retreat away from the concerns of church and state. This is where they would enjoy the life of country gentlemen amongst fishponds, orchards, gardens and parkland. The magnificent great hall was built by Henry de Gower, bishop from 1328 to 1347. Later additions include a Tudor chapel which has a very fine east window.
• Some three miles east of Pembroke, on the A4139.
Phone: 01646 672224
www.cadw.wales.gov.uk

St Govan's Chapel and St Justinian's. Sites relating to early Celtic Christianity are very much in evidence throughout Pembrokeshire. On the **Castlemartin peninsula,** St Govan, an Irish hermit, reputedly hid in a crevice in the rock, which miraculously opened for him. It is on this site that St Govan's Chapel was built. St Justinian's, near St David's, is the site of a medieval chapel and one of the area's many holy wells.
• For St Govan's Chapel, follow the B4319 southward from Pembroke, then take a narrow lane going left after St Petrox.

Preseli Hills

'Bluestone Country'. They are far from being Wales's highest summits, but the Preseli Hills nevertheless hold a powerful attraction. Said to hide the entrance to Annwn, the underworld of Celtic mythology, they are generally accepted to

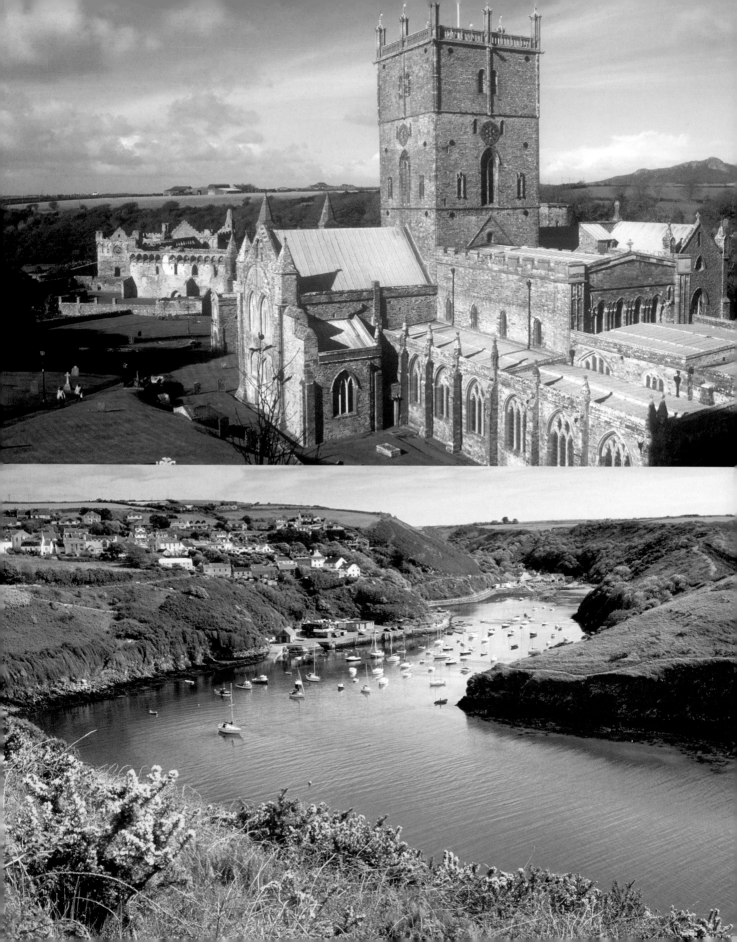

be the place from which the blue stones of Stonehenge were transported.

• From the B4313 and B4329, explore the minor roads over to Newport and Carningli.

Pentre Ifan Burial Chamber. In prehistoric times, the western extremities of Wales were at the centre of the sea routes linking what we now know as Scotland, Ireland and Brittany. Little wonder, then, that Pembrokeshire has so many cromlechs, standing stones and burial chambers. Pentre Ifan, situated on a gentle hill with wide views towards the sea, surely commemorates someone of great importance during those distant times.

• Signposted from the A487 between Newport and Felindre Farchog.
www.cadw.wales.gov.uk

Gwaun Valley. This tranquil place is a relic of the last Ice Age, when vast amounts of meltwater carved it out as the glaciers retreated. Pontfaen's small church is dedicated to St Brynach, a 6th century missionary who is said to have communed with angels on the summit of **Carningli** in the **Preseli Hills** above the valley. The area has a sense of mystery about it, heightened by the refusal, since the 18th century, of its inhabitants to accept modernisation of the calendar: New Year is celebrated hereabouts each January 13th.

• Follow the narrow road to Pontfaen from the B4313 south-east of Fishguard.

St David's

Saint David, the patron saint of Wales, was born around 462 AD on the site of the chapel named after his mother, St Non, near the little city that now bears his name. Following a lifetime of dedication to God, he came to be revered as a great Christian leader. The magnificent cathedral of St David's, built from the 12th century onwards, graces the secluded valley of the River Alun, where, despite being hidden from the sea, earlier churches were destroyed by Vikings. In contrast with the ascetic lifestyle of the Celtic saints, the medieval bishops of St David's enjoyed great wealth – the extravagant architecture of the Bishop's Palace reflects the status of Henry de Gower and his successors as major figures of church and state.

• Reach this westernmost part of Wales via the M4, A48, A40 and A487 – or by rail to Fishguard or Haverfordwest.
www.stdavids.co.uk

Porthclais, Abereiddi, Porthgain, Abercastle. With no railway within reach, the small ports of this far western coast were vital for the export of local slate, granite, and gravel for building and road making, and for the import of goods to sustain these remote communities. The last cargo of stone was shipped out from Porthgain in 1929, but the tiny harbour, with its rusting cranes, bollards and machinery, remains full of character.

• Between St David's and Fishguard, on minor roads that reward patience.

Solva

Of the small ports around **St Bride's Bay**, Solva grew to be the most important for fishing and for trade with Ireland, Bristol and elsewhere. Its zigzag entrance and narrow proportions provided excellent shelter and made it easy to defend against the Vikings. There was some small-scale shipbuilding here during the 19th century and there are the remains of several lime kilns at the harbour. Nowadays, it is a popular cruising destination for yacht owners, for whom negotiating the entrance – past the memorably named **St Elvis Rocks** – is a satisfying navigational exercise.

• Carefully negotiate the narrow roads down to the harbour from the A487 east of St David's.
www.solva.net

Middle Mill Woollen Mill, Solva. This mill has been in continuous production since it opened in 1907. Dyed and spun yarn is mainly woven into floor rugs and carpets.

Left:
Tenby Harbour. The scenic location and colourful buildings of Tenby's picturesque harbour, used by fishing boats and pleasure craft, have long attracted artists and holidaymakers.

Below:
Tudor Merchant's House. The Flemish influences on the Tudor Merchant's House in Tenby are evidence of how the long coastline of Wales has, for many centuries, opened the way for contact and trade with other countries.

The original waterwheel is undergoing restoration, and the machinery is now powered by electricity. The factory contains five Dobcross looms and their associated warping and wefting machinery.
• Just inland from Solva, along narrow lanes.
Phone: 01437 721112
www.solvawoollenmill.co.uk

....

Tenby

Picturesque Tenby has been one of the main tourism centres of Wales since the arrival of the railway in 1863, but the attractive town and cosy harbour, centred between two fabulous sandy beaches, were popular destinations for artists and travellers long before then. Tenby's origins are as a working port, one of the most important in Wales during the Middle Ages. The Norman presence, centred on the castle, generated trade with France, Spain and Portugal. Many buildings reflect the port's continuing prosperity during Tudor times as a centre for fishing and coal export. The Victorians realised, though, that it was in their interest to develop the town as a resort, and leisure boating, bathing and promenading gradually took over from commercial craft.
• Alive with holiday fun in summer, Tenby has all the resources of a popular resort, including excellent eating places.
www.visitpembrokeshire.com

Tenby Museum and Art Gallery. Founded in 1878, this is one of the oldest independent museums in Wales; it is run largely by an enthusiastic band of volunteers. The displays cover archaeology, geology, natural history and the maritime and social history of Tenby and south Pembrokeshire from the Stone Age to the present day. The **Wilfred Harrison Gallery** houses a collection of works by Augustus John, Gwen John, Nina Hamnet, EJ Head and other local artists.
Phone: 01834 842809
www.tenbymuseum.free-online.co.uk

Tenby Tudor Merchant's House. This late-15th century house is a fine example of a wealthy merchant's home, reflecting family life in Tudor times, when Tenby was a thriving port. The Flemish-style round chimney at the back is evidence of the presence of people from the Low Countries in southern Pembrokeshire at the time. The family would have lived on the first and second floors, with servants preparing food on the ground floor.
• On Quay Hill, off Tudor Square, close to the railway station and less than a mile (about 1.5km) from the Pembrokeshire Coast Path.
Phone: 01834 842279
www.nationaltrust.org.uk

....

Festivals and events

Newport Bay Spring Festival. This four-day sports, cultural and entertainment festival is held at Newport in northern Pembrokeshire over the early-**May** holiday. It features music, dance, arts and crafts exhibitions, cycling, walking, running, a mini regatta and horse riding events.
• Newport is on the A487 between Fishguard and Cardigan.
Phone: 01239 820912
www.newport-pembs.co.uk

Fishguard Folk Festival. Held at the end of **May**, this is a weekend of folk music, song and dance. Ever-increasing in popularity, it is being noticed more and more on a national stage. There are concerts, dance displays, meet the artist events, instrumental and voice workshops, informal music and song sessions, and a real ale bar.
• Venues include the Royal Oak pub and Theatr Gwaun, both of which have programmes and information.
Phone: 01348 875183
www.pembrokeshire-folk-music.co.uk/festival.htm

St David's Cathedral Festival. For nine days annually, in late **May** and early **June**, St David's Cathedral is host to a feast of classical music. The reverberant acoustics and inspiring architecture of the nave, including its 16th century Irish oak ceiling, provide a concert venue of rare atmosphere. Under the musical direction of cathedral organist Timothy Noon, the St David's Cathedral Choir and the Festival Orchestra combine their abilities with singers and instrumentalists representing a range of styles and eras.

• There are steep paths down from the square and more level access from the signed main entrance to the cathedral.
Phone: 01437 721682
www.stdavidscathedral.org.uk/festivals.htm

Pembrokeshire Fish Week. Late **June** sees a programme of more than 50 family-friendly events and activities around Pembrokeshire. In this food-lover's paradise, there are opportunities to try speciality fish and shellfish dishes, and to attend wine tastings and cookery demonstrations. There are also competitions for anglers – coarse, fly and sea – along with have-a-go sessions for newcomers.

• Upwards of 160 restaurants, food shops and pubs are involved in the food events; demonstrations by celebrity chefs are at the Torch Theatre, Milford Haven; angling is at Milford Haven (sea), Llawhaden Reservoir (coarse) and other inland waters.
Phone: 01437 776168
www.pembrokeshire.gov.uk/fishweek

Haverfordwest Festival Week. Held in early **July**, the week includes spectacular re-enactments by the Knights of the Longshanks – who, from their base at Haverfordwest Castle, sally forth into the town, taking hostage any unfortunate civic dignitary who crosses their path. Medieval battle re-enactments also take place at the castle and you may visit the medieval fayre, where a range of produce is sold, and see how the knights lived. There are also Victorian-themed events and the week ends with the Haverfordwest Carnival.
Phone: 01437 763427
www.haverfordwest-wales.info /com_ events.asp

Pembrokeshire Agricultural Show. In mid **August**, the Withybush Showground near Haverfordwest welcomes some 100,000 visitors to one of the largest regional agricultural shows in Wales. The three days of countryside activity and fun enthral local residents and visiting city dwellers alike. Animals ranging from cattle, sheep and horses to poultry, dogs and cage birds compete for honours. Vintage tractors, the Welsh Axe Team, sheepdog trials and show jumping add to the entertainment.

• Withybush is just north of Haverfordwest, on the A40.
Phone: 01437 764331
www.pembrokeshirecountyshow.co.uk

The Really Wild Food and Countryside Festival. With the botanist Professor David Bellamy as its patron, The Really Wild Food and Countryside Festival is a celebration of foods and countryside crafts that originate from the wild. Exhibition stands and demonstrations show how we can all explore, understand and make use of wild materials and ingredients in the same way that our ancestors did, but with some new ideas.

• Held at St David's Football Ground in early **September**.
Phone: 01348 891381
www.reallywildfestival.co.uk

Tenby Arts Festival. In combination with the attractiveness and historical interest of the town itself, this festival's programme of instrumental music, choral performances, talks, drama, art exhibitions, films, workshops and beach activities will ensure that a late-season break in Tenby will be enjoyable and memorable.

• Many of Tenby's churches, museums, galleries, restaurants, pubs and halls echo to the sounds of the festival's performances, and the applause of appreciative audiences, during late **September**.
Phone: 01834 845341
www.tenbyartsfest.co.uk

Right:
Wales's maritime traditions are brought to life during festivals and regattas in Pembrokeshire and elsewhere around the coast.

Below:
Pembrokeshire Fish Week. Food-lovers are well catered for with seafood extravaganzas, crab lunches, fish and chip suppers, seafood barbecues and the Fish and Shellfish Masterclass. Seafood tapas tastings, rock pool rambles, snorkel safari and children's angling open days are just some of the activities at this festival.

Carmarthenshire

Carmarthen, Carreg Cennen Castle, Dinefwr Park, Laugharne, Dolaucothi Gold Mines, the National Botanic Garden, Aberglasney, the National Wool Museum and the National Coracle Centre.

Above:
National Botanic Garden. The spectacular Great Glasshouse, designed by Foster & Partners, at the National Botanic Garden provides a favourable environment for tropical and desert plants.

Carmarthenshire towns. The main towns of the county vary enormously in character. Industrial **Llanelli**, in the south, was a prominent centre of tinplate production, an activity that continues there today. The **Millennium Coastal Park** has reclaimed many industrial sites for public enjoyment. **Burry Port** was built for the export of coal from the Gwendraeth valley, to which it was linked by rail. **Ammanford** grew as the main town of the western, anthracite-producing region of the great coalfield of southern Wales. **Llandeilo** and **Newcastle Emlyn**, in complete contrast, are historic market towns serving, respectively, the Tywi and Teifi valleys.
• The A-roads will get you around, but be sure to seek out minor routes.
www.carmartheshire.gov.uk

Carmarthen

To the Romans, Carmarthen was Moridunum, the Sea Fort, a secure place to import the supplies that sustained their presence in the region. The same imperative drove the Normans to build their castle overlooking the river. The town's Welsh name – **Caerfyrddin** – derives from Myrddin Emrys, Merlin the Magician, who is said to have been born here. During the Middle Ages, Carmarthen became one of the main market towns of Wales, its huddle of narrow streets crowded around the castle. It remains the regional administrative and shopping centre today. The imposing **County Hall**, in the style of a French chateau, dominates the view of the town from the river.
• Some fifteen miles from the western end of the M4 motorway, along the A48 dual carriageway.
www.carmarthenshire.gov.uk

Roman and Merlin connections.
Archaeological evidence of early settlement around Carmarthen includes the Iron Age hill fort at **Merlin's Hill**, Abergwili. Nature trails take you to the hilltop site where you may imagine Merlin enjoying the same

Left:
Dinefwr Castle.
The prominent fortress of Dinefwr is one of several castles that punctuate the green and gentle landscape of the Tywi Valley.

Below:
Carmarthenshire County Museum.
An £8 banknote of 1829, issued by The Carmarthen Bank of Walters, Jones and Co, from the collections of Carmarthenshire County Museum. The bank was bankrupt by 1832!.

views. In Carmarthen itself, the Roman amphitheatre was just one of the structures, along with forum, temple and baths, that were essential in a provincial town of substance.
Phone: 01267 237808
www.merlinshill.com

Oriel Myrddin Gallery. With its exhibits approved for quality by the Crafts Council, this regional gallery and crafts centre is well worth a visit. Open all year, it puts on an ever-changing programme of exhibitions, creative workshops and activities for all ages.
• Located in a listed Victorian art school in Church Lane, on the eastern side of the town, opposite St Peter's Church.
Phone: 01267 222775
www.carmarthenshire.gov.uk

Carmarthenshire County Museum.
The county's past is chronicled at this informative museum. The building was once the palace of the bishops of St David's, and it was here that the New Testament was first translated into Welsh in 1567. The displays feature prehistoric remains, Roman artefacts, landscape paintings, costume, decorative items, Welsh furniture and much more.
Don't miss the Victorian schoolroom and the carefully preserved remains of the ancient Carmarthen oak: Merlin the Magician was said to have prophesied that if this tree fell, so would the town.
• Set in delightful parkland at Abergwili, just off the A40 towards Llandeilo.
Phone: 01267 228696
www.carmarthenshire.gov.uk

Gwili Railway. This trip down memory lane starts at **Bronwydd Arms,** north of Carmarthen, and follows a section of the old Great Western line that once ran to Aberystwyth. For much of its route, the steam train runs alongside the **River Gwili,** passing through a pleasant farming landscape. At its terminus, **Llwyfan Cerrig,** where stone was once loaded from the

quarry that forms an impressive backdrop, there is a restored station building from **Felinfach**. You might also enjoy a ride on the miniature railway.
• Bronwydd Arms is some three miles north of Carmarthen, on the A484.
Phone: 01267 230666
www.gwili-railway.co.uk

Kidwelly

As early as 1223, there is a record of Henry III licensing one Robert de Cadwely, Magister Navis – ship's master – to trade wool and animal skins to France, and to bring back wine and olive oil. The 13th century castle and its great gatehouse, completed in 1422, are remarkably well preserved. Kidwelly gives an unusually complete insight into the evolution of a medieval fortress into an increasingly domesticated, though still very grand, household. By the 19th century, when coal mining boomed in the **Gwendraeth valley** inland, ships had grown to a size that the silt-prone estuary could not handle and the town has retained its compact charm.
• Ten miles south of Carmarthen, on the A484.
www.kidwelly.gov.uk

Kidwelly Industrial Museum. Wales once produced much of the world's tinplate, which was used for the tin cans that were such a leap forward in food storage during the 19th century. Llanelli grew to be the largest centre of production but there was also a **tinplate works**, set in attractive countryside, at Kidwelly. It is now home to a fascinating museum, which also describes other industries including coal mining and brick making that evolved in this largely rural county.
• From the A484 Kidwelly bypass, follow signs for Mynydd-y-Garreg.
Phone: 01554 891078
www.carmarthenshire.gov.uk

Left:
The Boathouse at Laugharne.
It is little wonder that Dylan Thomas was inspired to such flights of genius in his descriptions of sea and coastline. This is where he lived and worked.

Below:
Aberglasney.
Small but perfectly formed, the gardens of Aberglasney are within easy reach of the National Botanic Garden. These remarkable attractions provide two excellent reasons to visit Carmarthenshire.

Laugharne

Dylan Thomas and his wife Caitlin first moved here in 1938, a year after getting married, and returned to settle at **The Boathouse** in 1948. The **Dylan Thomas Trail** will lead you to many sites associated with Wales's greatest English-language poet – in Carmarthenshire, Swansea, Pembrokeshire and Ceredigion. His presence still pervades Laugharne. He would work intensively in his writing shed above **The Boathouse** (now a museum to his life and work) before adjourning to his favoured drinking haunt, **Brown's Hotel,** in the village. Dylan and Caitlin are buried in **St Martin's churchyard,** their grave marked by a simple white cross. Inside the church is a replica of the memorial stone to him in Poet's Corner, Westminster Abbey.
• Laugharne is on the A4066, four miles south of St Clears. Walk along roads and paths familiar to Dylan Thomas.
www.laugharne.co.uk

Llansteffan Castle. Sunset is a great time to visit **Ferryside**, on the eastern shore of the **Towy estuary**, to savour the romantic sight of the ruins of **Llansteffan Castle** high on the cliff-top opposite. Established in the early 12th century, on the site of an Iron Age promontory fort, it was held by the de Camville family of Norman barons for much of the Middle Ages.
• Follow minor roads west from Kidwelly, with great views of the Gwendraeth estuary.
www.cadw.wales.gov.uk

West Wales Centre for the Crafts. Located at **St Clears**, this multi-role centre has a large gallery featuring work by local artists, several of whom work in the associated studios and workshops. It also has a coffee-house restaurant. Check out the events programme for talks and tuition in a range of creative activities.
• St Clears is nine miles west of Carmarthen, on the A40 dual carriageway.
www.artswales.org

Llandeilo

Llandeilo is a small, but thriving, market town in Carmarthenshire, situated on the edge of the Brecon Beacons National Park. Llandeilo is named after one of the most eminent and celebrated Celtic saints of the 6th century, Saint Teilo, who established a small monastic settlement on the site of the present day church. Its narrow streets and historic buildings make this an attractive town. The bridge over the River Towy was built in 1848 and is the largest single span stone bridge in Wales.

Dinefwr Park and Newton House. Just west of Llandeilo, this medieval deer park, delightfully landscaped and extended in 1775 by **Lancelot "Capability" Brown**, is home to around a hundred fallow deer and a small herd of an ancient breed of long-horned white cattle. Walks lead to **Dinefwr Castle**, stronghold of the Lord Rhys, from which there are wide views of the gentle **Tywi valley**. Newton House, built in 1660 but now with a Victorian Gothic Revival façade and fountain garden, contains an exhibition about its history and a tea room with views of the deer park.
• A short drive or a moderate walk from the centre of Llandeilo.
Phone: 01558 824512
www.nationaltrust.org.uk

Aberglasney. The 15th century bard Lewis Glyn Cothi wrote of a white-painted house here, surrounded by nine gardens, orchards, vineyards and large oak trees. It was one of the earliest descriptions of any house and garden in Wales. In the subsequent ownership of the Bishop of St David's and a series of wealthy families, the estate was enlarged and improved, but its fortunes eventually declined and it became derelict. Since 1995, the Aberglasney Restoration Trust has worked hard to reverse this sorry fate and "The Garden Lost in Time" is once again amongst Wales's finest gardens. The intriguing yew tunnel, believed to be over a thousand years old,

and many 16th and 17th century features have survived.
• Off the A40 west of Llandeilo and close to the National Botanic Garden.
Phone: 01558 668998
www.aberglasney.org

Iron-Age fort at Garn Goch, near Bethlehem. One of the largest Iron Age hill forts in Wales stands 700 feet (213m) above sea level in the Brecon Beacons National Park. Its extensive ramparts follow the contours of the hill. The ravages of the past two thousand years have reduced them to lines of rubble but they once stood tall and would have been a daunting sight. Bethlehem – named, as are many Welsh villages, after its chapel – sees many visitors in the weeks before Christmas, when its seasonal post office opens for the franking of cards and the sale of commemorative covers.
• Signposted along a minor road heading north-eastwards from Llandeilo.

Carreg Cennen Castle. Few castles anywhere command a location as spectacular or as difficult to attack as this. On its precipitous 320 foot (100m) limestone crag, in the far west of the Brecon Beacons National Park, this atmospheric stronghold is evocative of legend or fairy tale. Its origins are obscure but it fell alternately into Welsh and English hands during the Middle Ages, before being largely dismantled in 1462. A visit is made all the more memorable if you descend the dark and narrow passageway leading to a small natural cave beneath the fortifications, which was possibly inhabited during prehistoric times. It would have been an uncomfortable hideaway for non-combatants as battle raged above.
• Follow signs to Trapp and the castle from the A483 south of Llandeilo.
Phone: 01558 822291
www.cadw.wales.co.uk

Dryslwyn Castle and Paxton's Tower. Recent excavation has uncovered much evidence concerning this hilltop defensive site. Originally a castle of the native Welsh princes of Deheubarth, it was taken by the forces of Edward I in 1287, but returned to Welsh hands – those of Owain Glyndŵr – in 1403. Nearby Paxton's Tower was built in 1811 as a monument to Lord Nelson and provides a tremendous elevated viewpoint.
• Five miles west of Llandeilo along the A40/B4300.
www.cadw.wales.gov.uk
www.nationaltrust.org.uk

National Botanic Garden of Wales. This is a national treasure for the whole of the UK. It is a botanic garden in the full sense, being a centre for research as well as a gloriously attractive place to enjoy flowers, plants and trees. Built on the once-neglected Middleton estate, where the fine house burned down in 1931, the gardens include the sheltered double-walled garden, original water features, many new plantings and the Wallace Garden, honouring the famous Welsh botanist Alfred Russell Wallace. The National Botanic Garden also boasts the world's largest single span glasshouse and one of Europe's longest herbaceous borders, all set within a partially restored Regency Park.
• Easily reached via its own junction on the A48, close to the western end of the M4.
www.gardenofwales.org.uk
Phone: 01558 668768

Talley Abbey. This was the only abbey in Wales to be founded by the Premonstratensians, or White Canons, whose way of life combined Cistercian and Augustinian principles. It was founded for them by their supporter Lord Rhys ap Gruffudd late in the 12th century, but it was poorly funded and never became a leading religious house.
• Idyllically situated on the B4302 north of Llandeilo.
www.cadw.wales.gov.uk

Right:
Carreg Cennen Castle. On its thrilling clifftop site, Carreg Cennen Castle occupies one of the best defensive positions in the whole of Wales.

Below:
National Botanic Garden of Wales. Working with the National Museum Wales and the Countryside Council for Wales, the National Botanic Garden is conserving some of Wales's rarest flowers and trees, and the Great Glasshouse is a refuge for some of the world's most endangered plants.

Llandovery

Park beneath the castle and admire the remarkable stainless steel sculpture of **Llywelyn ap Gruffydd Fychan**, loyal supporter of Owain Glyndŵr, then call at the Heritage Centre, with its statue of a cattle drover outside. Along the street is the **memorial church to William Williams of Pantycelyn**. He was a poet, a preacher and the best-loved of Welsh hymn writers. Of more than nine hundred hymns penned by him, 'Guide Me O Thou Great Redeemer' is perhaps the most familiar and inspiring, whether it is sung in competent four-part harmony by a Welsh congregation or roared by tens of thousands of rugby supporters in the emotional cauldron of Cardiff's Millennium Stadium.
• From the M4, follow the A483 and A40 to the inland part of Carmarthenshire.

Dolaucothi Gold Mines. The appeal of western Wales to the Romans derived largely from the minerals they extracted here which included a substantial quantity of gold, likely to have been transported under heavy guard to the empire's mints in Lyon and Rome. They left some two kilometres of underground workings at Dolaucothi, near Pumsaint, a site that was mined again in the 19th and 20th centuries, and continues occasionally to be explored for possibilities. Guided tours take you through Roman and more recent tunnels, and you may experience the frustrations of prospectors as you attempt to pan for gold.
• Off the A482 mid-way between Llandovery and Lampeter.
Phone: 01558 650177
www.nationaltrust.org.uk

Llanelli

Historically a minor town on the mouth of the River Loughor, Llanelli grew significantly in the 18th and 19th centuries with the mining of coal and later the tinplate industry. It became such a significant regional producer of tin that it was referred to as "Tinopolis" by the latter half of the 19th century. The closure of coal mines and competition from overseas steel plants meant that Llanelli, like many other towns in south Wales saw significant and sustained economic decline from the late 1970s. Today, Llanelli is an attractive town with a proud rugby tradition.

Llanelli Millennium Coastal Park. Occupying 20 kilometres of coastline along the Burry Estuary, Llanelli's Millennium Coastal Park looks across to the scenic Gower Peninsula. It features a range of leisure attractions and natural habitats, linked by a coastal path and cycleway extending from The National Wetlands Centre Wales, at Penclacwydd, to Pembrey Country Park.

Theatr Elli, Llanelli, and The Lyric, Carmarthen. Regional theatre is alive and well in Wales, with venues such as these putting on lively progammes of theatre, music, comedy, films and other entertainment in both English and Welsh.
• Programmes in local newspapers and from Tourist Information Centres.
Phone: 0845 226 3509 (Lyric)
Phone: 0845 226 3508 (Elli)
www.carmarthenshiretheatres.co.uk

Newcastle Emlyn

National Coracle Centre, Cenarth. Here, the river Teifi tumbles over the impressive **Cenarth Falls**, one of Wales's first tourist attractions, much visited by Victorian travellers. The National Coracle Centre, which is housed in a 17th century flour mill that is driven by a water wheel, has an international collection of coracles from as far afield as America, India, Vietnam, Tibet and Iraq. The local version evolved as a lightweight one-man craft suited to netting salmon and trout on the rapid waters of the Teifi.
• Three miles west of Newcastle Emlyn, on the A484 towards Cardigan.
Phone: 01239 710980
www.coracle-centre.co.uk

Left and below: **National Wool Museum.** Every aspect of the production of wool in its varied forms is explained at this museum.

Below left: **Merlin Magic and Mystery Festival.** This Arthurian festival brings a touch of magic to Carmarthen with medieval re-enactors, stuntmen, jesters and magicians.

National Wool Museum, Drefach Felindre. At the restored Cambrian Mills near Newcastle Emlyn, discover the fascinating history of the Welsh woollen industry, which was a vital contributor to the economy in many parts of Wales. Experience the clatter of the complicated machinery, hear the stories of the mill workers, and see the cloth in all its richly coloured and patterned glory. This fine museum, part of the National Museum Wales, also features items from the national textile collection. There is something for everyone to enjoy: you can even try your hand at carding, spinning and sewing.
• Some twelve miles north of Carmarthen, on the A484.
www.museumwales.ac.uk

Pendine

Pendine Museum of Speed. Overlooking one of the longest and smoothest stretches of sand in the UK, the museum tells the story of the land speed record attempts and racing that went on there. The main exhibit is "Babs", the car used by Parry Thomas for his fatal attempt at the record in 1927. The car was buried in the sands for many years before being recovered and restored by enthusiasts.
• Continue along the A4066 from Laugharne until you reach the wide sands of Pendine.
Phone: 01994 453488
www.carmarthenshire.gov.uk

Hywel Dda Gardens and Interpretive Centre, Whitland. Hywel ap Cadell ruled much of Wales during the ninth and early tenth centuries. He devised a remarkably wise and humane legal system, which remained in force until Henry VIII's Act of Union with England in 1536. Hywel's emphasis on compensating the victim rather than punishing the offender, and his enlightened views on the rights of women earned him the name Hywel Dda, Howell the Good. This attractive garden in his memory is said to be the only one in Europe dedicated to the law.
• Five miles west of St Clear's on the A448 towards Haverfordwest.
Phone: 01994 240867
www.hywel-dda.co.uk

Festivals and events

United Counties Show. This two-day agricultural show, held each **August**, has drawn the crowds for more than a century. It promotes agriculture in west Wales through impressive livestock competitions in the main ring, a wide variety of stands and stalls, a craft marquee and a large food hall.
• Phone: 01267 232141
email: enquiries@unitedcounties.co.uk

Welsh Game Fair. Held in **June**, the Welsh Game Fair is an atmospheric gathering for country folk and all who enjoy the traditions of rural life, including working-dog enthusiasts and participants in shooting, fishing and equestrian pursuits. Held in the pleasant surroundings of Gelli Aur Country Park, the fair has a lively programme of events and a range of food and craft stalls.
• Phone: 01267 281410
email: wgftrade@talktalk.net

Merlin, Magic and Mystery Festival. Carmarthen steps back into its medieval past each **June**, with an array of entertainment including street performers, magicians, storytellers and medieval re-enactments. There is also a local arts and crafts market, live music and a parade. The festival brings to life the town's legendary connection with the Arthurian magician Merlin.
• Phone: 01554 747542
email: leisure@carmarthenshire.gov.uk

Swansea and Gower

The bustling city, the Swansea Valley and nearby Gower feature the Swansea Maritime Quarter, Margam Abbey, National Waterfront Museum, Glynn Vivian Gallery, Dylan Thomas Centre, Swansea Festival of Music and the Arts, Swansea Grand Theatre, and Brangwyn Hall.

Above:
Three Cliffs Bay. Getting to this marvellous place involves a moderate walk through sand dunes, from Southgate, but means that when you get there you will find no cars or buildings to spoil the view.

Cynonville

South Wales Miners' Museum. Located within the **Afan Argoed Countryside Centre**, this small but moving museum depicts the story of the miner and his family as they coped with the dangers of the job in the great coalfield of the south Wales Valleys. A range of outdoor exhibits includes a blacksmith's workshop.
• Exit J40 of the M4 to the A4107 and follow signs to Cymmer and Argoed Forest Park.
Phone: 01639 850564
www.npt.gov.uk

Gower

The Gower Peninsula. In 1956, Gower became the first place in Britain to be designated an Area of Outstanding Natural Beauty. Within its compact dimensions you will find spectacular cliffs, magnificent beaches, elevated heathland, lush meadows, oak woods, salt marshes and sand dunes. Rich evidence of human habitation – including Neolithic and Bronze Age sites, medieval castles, ancient hedgerows and farm boundaries, and 18th century parkland – underlines its appeal through the centuries. Former fishing villages, including Mumbles and Port Eynon, have become popular holiday and leisure destinations.
• Head westward from Swansea on the A4118 – or follow the walking and cycling route around Swansea Bay to Mumbles.

Gower Heritage Centre, Parkmill. The whole family can learn all about the rural life of Gower at this entertaining attraction. Parkmill is a water-powered cornmill and sawmill where you will find farm animals, mini-tractor rides and a puppet theatre.
• On the A4118, a couple of miles past Swansea airport.
Phone: 01792 371206
www.gowerheritagecentre.co.uk

Above left:
Mumbles.
Renowned for its fine restaurants and seafront café culture.

Above:
Weobley Castle.
Better described as a fortified manor house than a fortress, Weobley Castle was built as an elegant residence for the de la Bere family.

Left:
Margam Country Park. A great place to enjoy scenic beauty, history and wildlife.

The Castles of Gower. Oystermouth is the finest of Gower's castles. It was founded by William de Londres early in the 12th century and became the main residence of the de Braose family, Lords of Gower. **Loughor Castle** has a 13th century tower on top of a 12th century earthwork, built on the corner of a Roman fort. **Weobley Castle** is a picturesque medieval fortified manor house with substantial remains dating from the early 14th century. **Oxwich Castle** consists of the remains of a sumptuous, mock-fortified manor built by the Mansel family during the 16th century.

• Follow the A4067 to Mumbles for Oystermouth. The A4118 takes you into Gower from Swansea.
www.cadw.wales.gov.uk

Margam

Margam Abbey. Set in 1000 acres of glorious parkland, Margam Country Park offers a variety of wildlife as well as a magnificent 18th century Orangery, monastic gardens and an impressive Tudor-Gothic style Victorian Mansion House which was built between 1830 and 1840. In its beautiful parkland surroundings, Margam Abbey Church (founded in 1147) is the only Cistercian foundation in Wales where the nave is intact and still used for Christian worship. Other remains of the original monastery include a twelve-sided chapter house in early-English style. The excellent **Margam Abbey Stones Museum** holds a small but very significant collection of inscribed Celtic and Roman stones and crosses, some of which were found within the local area, and includes the great **Wheel Cross of Conbelin**.

• Close to J38 on the M4 motorway.
Phone: 01639 871184
www.cadw.wales.gov.uk

Mumbles

Mumbles is one the UK's most attractive coastal towns. As early as 1806, a railway was built between Oystermouth and

Swansea. Initially this was to carry coal in horse-drawn trucks, but the novel idea of transporting people was soon seized upon and the first passenger railway service in the world began here in March 1807. Steam trains were later introduced and Mumbles became a popular day out. The line was extended and in 1898 the pier was constructed to serve as its new terminus. Mumbles has a good showing of craft shops.
• The A4067 and the bayside walking and cycle route are pleasing approaches.
www.visitswanseabay.com

Arthur's Stone. The capstone of this neolithic tomb on the summit of **Cefn-y-Bryn** weighs over twenty-five tons but legend has it that it was a pebble from King Arthur's shoe, thrown across the Burry Estuary. The stone is also said to make the journey to **Three Cliffs Bay** every New Year's Eve to drink from the sea.
• Seek out a local map showing paths to Cefn-y-bryn from Nicholaston on the A4118.

Neath

Neath Abbey. Originally founded as a daughter house of Savigny in 1130, Neath Abbey was absorbed into the Cistercian order in 1147 and was described as the 'Fairest Abbey in all Wales' by the Tudor historian John Leland. The site has enjoyed varying fortunes, even serving as an early copper works after dissolution. Situated near an industrial area, the abbey's location on the banks of the **Tennant Canal** makes it a tranquil place to visit.
• From J43 on the M4, follow signs for Skewen and the Abbey.
www.cadw.wales.gov.uk

Neath Canal. This scenic example of one of the main means of transport during the Industrial Revolution was made famous by the novelist Alexander Cordell in 'Song of the Earth.' Today, passenger craft navigate the restored section of the canal north of Resolven. The **'Enfys'**, a purpose-built boat for the disabled, is available for charter

and the **'Thomas Dadford'**, a twelve-seater trip boat, operates from Neath. The canal's towpath provides a great walk to Aberdulais, where the basin has a skew bridge and a twelve-arch aqueduct over the River Neath.
• Aberdulais and Resolven are north-east of Neath, on the A465.
www.waterscape.com/neathcanal

Neath Museum and Art Gallery. Situated in the town centre, this museum's two galleries cover the archaeology and natural history of the Neath area. Call in to meet Sebastian, the Roman soldier, who will tell you how tough life was in Neath's Roman fort, or try your hand at grinding corn.
• Approach from J41 or J44.
Phone: 01639 645726
www.npt.gov.uk/museums

Pontardawe Arts Centre. Pontardawe Arts Centre has gained a reputation as a fine cultural venue. The theatre hosts professional work of the highest calibre, from classical music to drama and dance, literature and children's theatre to blues and world music: something for everyone to enjoy. Regular cinema showings provide the opportunity to enjoy the latest blockbusters as well as the less mainstream art-house movies provided by the local film society. **Oriel Lliw Gallery** is the place to while away the time at the regular exhibitions. **Pontardawe Folk Festival**, an annual celebration of world music and dance with, as you might expect, a strong Celtic representation, is held in the town each August.
• Follow the A4067 from J45 on the M4.
Phone: 01792 863722
www.npt.gov.uk/pontardawe artscentre

Cefn Coed Colliery Museum. Wonder at the harsh life of the collier underground as you view the magnificent steam winding engine, the simulated coal-mine gallery and the displays of mining tools and equipment at this museum housed in the original buildings of the former Cefn Coed Colliery. Miner's lamps and other

Right:
Neath Abbey. Graceful Gothic arches hint at the past splendour of Neath Abbey, a place of tangible sanctity in a region of earthly endeavour and industry.

Far right:
Arthur's Stone. Central Gower is a maze of country lanes and paths – Arthur's Stone is a highlight.

Below:
Resolven Neath Canal. The towpaths of the Neath Canal lead past fascinating sites of industrial heritage, now restored to green again.

Left and above:
Swansea Marina.
The Maritime
Quarter is enlivened
by entertaining
public art – this
sculpture of blind
Captain Cat,
Dylan Thomas's
memorable
character from
Under Milk Wood,
stands on the
quayside at
Swansea Marina.

Above right:
Swansea city centre.
Swansea's bustling
city centre has
numerous
restaurants and
bars offering world
cuisine and fine
wines.

souvenirs are sold at the gift shop.
• At Crynant, north of Neath on the A4109.
Phone: 01639 750556
www.npt.gov.uk/museums

....

Swansea

Swansea's Maritime Quarter. Former docklands have been redeveloped to give Swansea one of the most attractive waterfronts you will find anywhere, all within a few minutes' walk of the city centre. The grand headquarters of the Swansea Harbour Trust, built in 1902, is now the five-star Morgan's boutique hotel, a comfortable stopover favoured by stars of stage, screen and sport, and a great place for a snack or a meal in the fine restaurant.
The Pumphouse, which once housed the steam engines that provided hydraulic power for the swing bridge, dock gates, cranes and dockside machinery nearby is a pub and restaurant. The impressive **National Waterfront Museum** is the place to learn all about the industrial, maritime

and social history of the whole of Wales.
• Between the shopping area and the beach. Underpasses and footbridges will get you past the busy seafront road.

Glynn Vivian Gallery. Make your way here to view a broad spectrum of visual art including works by old masters and by modern painters and sculptors. There is an internationally renowned collection of porcelain and Swansea pottery.
• On Alexandra Road.
Phone: 01792 516900
www.swansea.gov.uk

Egypt Centre. University of Wales Swansea, is one of the most popular centres in the UK for the study of Egyptology, and this centre, which is open to the public, gives an authoritative introduction to the dynasties that once ruled along the Nile.
• The university occupies a large campus at Singleton Park, west of the city centre.
Phone: 01790 295960
www.swan.ac.uk/egypt

National Waterfront Museum. The story of Wales at work in industries old and new is brought to life by fascinating exhibits and informative multimedia presentations at this superb new museum in **Swansea's Maritime Quarter**. A tremendous selection of items is on display, from wonderful paintings and intricate ship models to large vehicles and powerful machinery; from precious decorative art to the collar worn by the famous life-saving dog Swansea Jack; and from the hand tools of traditional trades to examples of today's groundbreaking technologies. You will also find a shop and a café in the quayside warehouse, linked to a spectacular new gallery clad in Welsh slate, in which the museum is housed.
• Car parks nearby.
Phone: 01792 638950
www.museumwales.ac.uk

Swansea Grand Theatre. At the heart of the city, this charming theatre presents over five hundred performances a year in all styles of entertainment from comedy to classical music, drama to ballet, opera to the much-loved traditional Christmas pantomime. The Arts Wing hosts exhibitions and the Rooftop Cafe Bar is a dramatic meeting place.
• In the main shopping area, conveniently close to train and bus stations and car parks.
Phone: 01792 475715
www.swanseagrand.co.uk

Taliesin Arts Centre. Owned and managed by the University of Wales Swansea, Taliesin Arts Centre is a very popular venue presenting a wide variety of performances and exhibitions. It is named after Taliesin, the 6th century Celtic bard. Over the past twenty years, the programme of activities and events has grown to include regular cinema screenings, an average of ten visiting exhibitions per year, and a great variety of live performances from dance and drama to jazz and world music.
• Phone: 01792 602060
www.taliesinartscentre.co.uk

National Waterfront Museum. Information technology of the entertaining and visitor-friendly variety is put to helpful use in describing and interpreting the themes explored at Swansea's National Waterfront Museum.

Far left:
Swansea Museum.
This traditional
museum of local
history is a short
walk from the
National Waterfront
Museum.

Left:
Swansea Festival.
A packed
programme of
events each
summer includes
everything from
colourful carnival
processions to
musical and
theatrical
performances at
the highest level.

Below:
**Dylan Thomas
Centre.** Visit this
exhibition to see
how growing up in
Swansea helped
shape the great
poet's destiny.

Swansea Museum. This is a traditional museum of local history where you will find display cases filled with fascinating exhibits. There is an Egyptian mummy and a 'Cabinet of Curiosities' packed with the sort of thing that intrigued the Victorians, including a preserved Dodo. A superb collection of toys and games will bring back many memories, and there are exquisite examples of Swansea and Nantgarw pottery.
• Opposite the end of Wind Street and a short walk from the National Waterfront Museum.
Phone: 01792 653763
www.swanseaheritage.net

Dylan Thomas Centre. Born at Cwmdonkin Drive in the Uplands area, the son of an English teacher at Swansea Grammar School, Dylan Thomas was prodigiously talented with words and became the most famous of all Welsh poets working in the English language. The Dylan Thomas Centre has an exhibition about his life and work, and an excellent bookshop-café. Pick up a leaflet for the trail to his birthplace and visit other significant locations including nearby **Cwmdonkin Park** where he played as a child and later found inspiration for poetry.
• Between the National Waterfront Museum and the Sail Bridge.
Phone: 01792 463980
www.dylanthomas.org

Swansea Castle. The remains of Swansea Castle are now dwarfed by the modern buildings that surround them, but a fine fortress once dominated the harbour below. Sailing ships used to dry out and unload at the estuary of the River Tawe – the foreshore was once much closer than it is today. The remains of the castle's tower date back to the late 13th century: the distinctive arcaded parapet, added later, is reminiscent of the episcopal palaces at **Lamphey** and **St David's**.
• Near the top of Wind Street, overlooking the city's main shopping area.
www.cadw.wales.gov.uk

Brangwyn Hall. This excellent concert hall, often used for broadcasting and recording, is decorated by a series of enormous and colourful murals depicting scenes from the British Empire. They were originally painted by Sir Frank Brangwyn for the House of Lords, but having been deemed rather too visually prominent for that building they were found an appreciative home here. The Brangwyn Hall is part of Swansea's impressive Civic Centre, built in Art Deco style during the 1930s.
• A short drive or bus ride to the west of the shopping area, towards the university.
Phone: 01792 635489
www.swansea.gov.uk

Festivals and events

Dylan Thomas Festival. Beginning on his birthday, the 27th of **October**, and ending on the anniversary of his death, the 9th of **November** – as the autumn nights draw in over the streets of his 'ugly lovely town' – Swansea celebrates the life and work of the city's most famous son. The **Dylan Thomas Centre** and the nearby **Dylan Thomas Theatre** are focal points for a full programme of readings, lectures and celebrations around the city.
• Details from the Dylan Thomas Centre.
Phone: 01792 463980
www.dylanthomas.com

Swansea's festivals. From **May** to **September** during the **Swansea Bay Summer Festival**, the city and its environs are alive to music and entertainment of all kinds, including the **Proms in the Park** concerts, open-air **Shakespeare at Oystermouth Castle**, and a host of children's events. The **National Transport Festival of Wales** and the **Maritime and Sea Shanty Festival** are part of the fun. The **Swansea Festival of Music and the Arts**, held each **October**, is one of Wales's major regional festivals; it offers a wealth of classical music at the highest standards of performance.
• Details from the Tourist Information Centre near the bus station.
www.swanseabayfestival.net

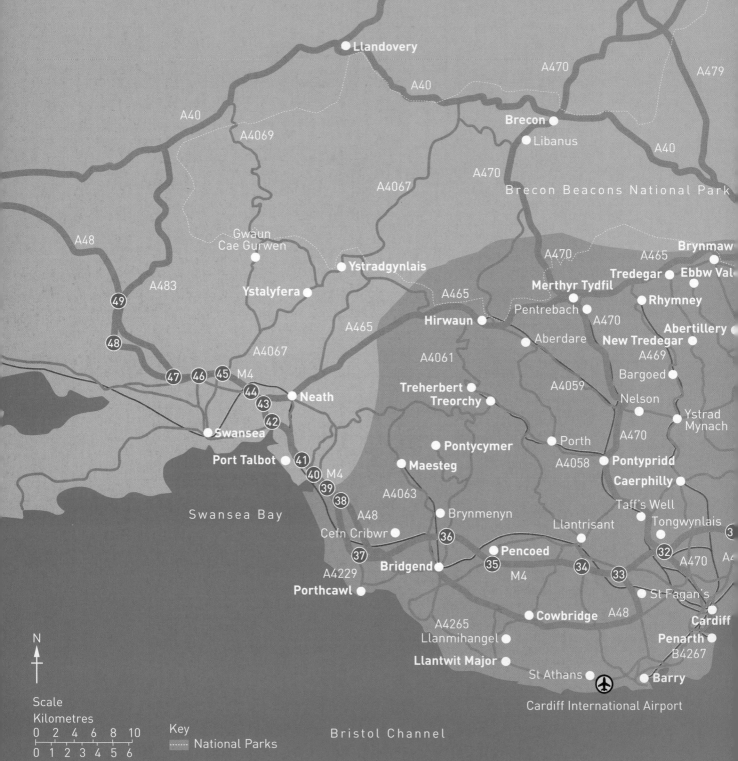

South East Wales

Llandovery

A40

A470

A479

A40

A4069

Brecon

Libanus

A40

A470

A40

A4067

Brecon Beacons National Park

A48

Gwaun
Cae Gurwen

Ystradgynlais

Brynmaw

A470

A465

A483

Ystalyfera

Merthyr Tydfil

Tredegar

Ebbw Val

49

A465

Pentrebach

Rhymney

Hirwaun

A470

Abertillery

48

Aberdare

New Tredegar

A4067

A465

A4061

A469

Bargoed

47   46   45   M4

Treherbert

A4059

Nelson

44

Treorchy

Ystrad
Mynach

43

Neath

42

Pontycymer

Porth

A470

Swansea

Maesteg

A4058   Pontypridd

Port Talbot   41

Caerphilly

40   M4

A4063

Taff's Well

39

Tongwynlais

38

Brynmenyn

Llantrisant

32

Swansea Bay

A48

Pencoed

A470

Cefn Cribwr

36

34

33

St Fagan's

37

35

Bridgend

M4

A4229

Cardiff

Porthcawl

Cowbridge   A48

Penarth

A4265

B4267

Llanmihangel

Llantwit Major

St Athans

Barry

Cardiff International Airport

N

Bristol Channel

Scale
Kilometres
0 2 4 6 8 10
0 1 2 3 4 5 6
Miles

Key
National Parks

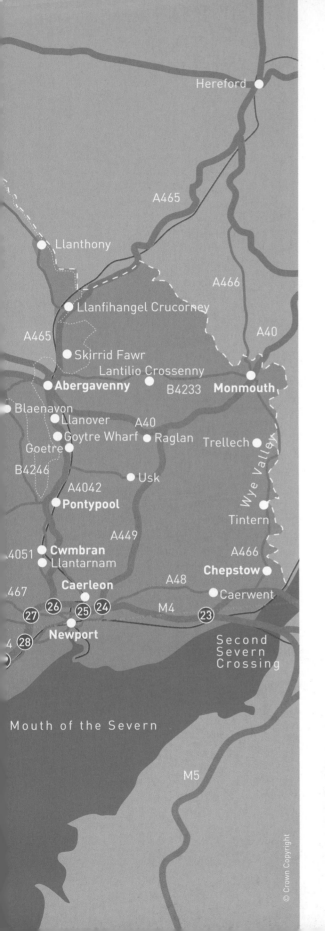

Welcome to south-east Wales, where cosmopolitan style meets traditional values. The formerly industrial Valleys are known the world over for their culture and heritage. The gentle Vale of Glamorgan is a region of quaint villages and historic towns. Cardiff, the capital city of Wales, oozes style and a cutting-edge dynamism that amazes visitors. The peace and tranquillity of the Wye Valley and the Vale of Usk are a far cry from the sounds of border warfare that echoed here for centuries.

GLAMORGAN COLLIERY LLWYNYPIA

South Wales Valleys

These cauldrons of industry and culture give us Blaenavon World Heritage Site, Rhondda Heritage Park, Caerphilly Castle, Llancaiach Fawr Manor, the Monmouthshire and Brecon Canal, Llantarnam Abbey, Blaenavon Book Town, the Cordell Museum, the Parc and Dare Miners' Institute and Cyfarthfa Castle.

Above:
Llwynypia miners.
Some of the youngsters in this picture of coal miners at Llwynypia look suspiciously clean in comparison with the men in the background, though boys as young as 15 worked underground – operating gates that directed the air flowing through the mine, rather than doing heavy work at the coalface itself.

Above:
Cynon Valley Museum. Learn about the social history of this highly populated and industrious region, including the tough working conditions and legendary camaraderie of the coal-mining communities.

Aberdare

Coliseum Theatre. Built in 1937, this striking building nestles in the residential Mount Pleasant Street in Aberdare. The auditorium is distinctive, with its acoustic nodules and intriguing wall friezes. The programme includes music and drama of all kinds, including productions by local community groups and schools.
• Aberdare is on the A4059, which extends north-westward from the A470 north of Pontypridd.
Phone: 01685 881188

Cynon Valley Museum. On the outskirts of Aberdare, you will find this museum of local social history, which also has a contemporary arts and crafts gallery with a changing exhibition programme. There is a café and a shop specialising in design-led jewellery, ceramics and glass.
• On the outskirts of the town, ten minutes' walk from the train and bus stations.
Phone: 01685 886729
www.cynonvalley.co.uk/cv_museum

Abertillery

St Illtyd's Church, Abertillery. This restored medieval church is a reminder that the history of this part of Wales is not exclusively to do with coal mining; there were people here long before that particular industry boomed. The simple exterior and enchanting interior of the church reflect the spiritual intentions of its builders, the white-robed Cistercian monks of nearby Llantarnam Abbey.
• From J28 on the M4, head northward on the A467, or drive southward on the same road from the A465 at Brynmawr.
Phone: 01495 355537
www.illtyd.abelalways.co.uk

Blaenavon

Blaenavon UNESCO World Heritage Site. Built in the 1780s, the Blaenavon ironworks was at the cutting edge of the new

Left:
Caerphilly Castle.
The intimidating defences, including the wide moat, would make any but the most determined of attackers think twice. The leaning tower seems to defy gravity.

Below:
Big Pit: National Coal Museum. The pithead winding gear, once a common sight throughout the mining valleys, continues to operate at this exciting museum.

technology that made the Industrial Revolution possible. A row of five blast furnaces, powered by steam, was served by an ingenious water-balanced system for transporting iron ore, coal and limestone into their open tops. Molten iron ran down to be cast into rows of 'pigs' in the yard below. Next to this place of hot and strenuous labour are the cottages of **Stack Square**, where workers lived in the shadow of the tall chimney.
• Go northward from Newport on the A4042, then take the A4043 from Pontypool, or head over the Blorenge mountain on the B4246 from Abergavenny.
Phone: 01495 792615
www.world-heritage-blaenavon.org.uk

Big Pit: National Coal Museum.
Situated within the **Blaenavon World Heritage Site**, Big Pit is a deep coalmine where you may descend three hundred feet underground in the cage that once took the miners to work. A former collier will explain to you, from first-hand experience, what life was like for the thousands of men who once toiled at the coal face. Big Pit won the Gulbenkian Prize for Museum of the Year in 2005.
• The industrial heritage sites of Blaenavon are a substantial distance apart and it is best to drive between them or join a tour.
Phone: 01495 790311
www.museumwales.ac.uk

Blaenavon Community Heritage and Cordell Museum. The **World Heritage Site of Blaenavon** is home to this substantial museum, where the displays will guide you through the history of the town from the Industrial Revolution to the modern day. The novelist Alexander Cordell wrote evocatively of life in this corner of Wales, and his desk, personal effects and typewriter may be seen here. Following the inspiration of Hay-on-Wye, Blaenavon's new role as a book town means that you will find a treasure trove of books old and new in its specialist shops.
• The museum is located in the town

centre and within reach of the bookshops.
Phone: 01495 790991
www.world-heritage-blaenavon.org.uk

Brynmawr

Brinore Tramroad. This is the eight-mile tram route, near Brynmawr, built in 1815 to link the enormous limestone quarry at Trefil to the **Monmouthshire and Brecon Canal** at Talybont.
• Take a minor road northward from the A465, three miles west of Brynmawr.
www.brinore-tramroad.powys.org.uk

Caerphilly

Caerphilly Castle. This is the largest medieval castle in Wales and, after Windsor and Dover, the third largest in Britain. It was built in the late-13th century by the Anglo-Norman lord of Glamorgan, Gilbert de Clare, to resist attack by supporters of the Welsh Prince Llywelyn. It is a supreme example of 'walls-within-walls' construction. Its water defences are remarkable: the moat widens into lakes that contain three artificial islands, and made the castle virtually impregnable. The famous leaning tower leans at a greater angle than that of Pisa. Look out for days when battle re-enactment societies bring history to life with glinting armour, clashing swords and replicas of ancient siege engines that hurl massive rocks long distances into the moat.
• Caerphilly is just north of Cardiff via the A469 or A470, then A468 from Nantgarw.
www.cadw.wales.gov.uk

Llantarnam

Llantarnam Abbey. Located near Cwmbran, Llantarnam is a working abbey, home to the Sisters of St Joseph of Annecy who welcome visitors by prior arrangement. It was originally built for a Cistercian community of monks in 1179, as a daughter house of Strata Florida. The remains of the original abbey are built into the present buildings; the large barn is especially impressive.

• From the M4 at J25a or J26, follow signs for Cwmbran to the roundabout on the A4051, then take a minor road signposted to Llantarnam.
Phone: 01633 483232

Merthyr Tydfil

Cyfarthfa Castle. This grand castellated mansion was commissioned by ironmaster William Crawshay in 1824. The area around Merthyr Tydfil and Dowlais was the largest iron-producing centre in the world. Crawshay's Cyfarthfa Ironworks produced cannon and cannon balls for the Royal Navy, including many used by Nelson's ships at Trafalgar in 1805. Large quantities of iron flowed from the furnaces to support the accelerating industrialisation of Britain and to make possible the spread of the emerging railway network. The **Cyfarthfa Castle Museum and Art Gallery** has a fine collection of paintings, decorative items and musical instruments.
• Cyfarthfa Castle is visible in all its grandeur from the A470 south of the junction with the A465 heads-of-the-valleys road, from which it may be reached.
Phone: 01685 723112
www.merthyr.gov.uk

Monmouthshire and Brecon Canal

This scenic canal runs for thirty-two miles (51km) from the **Brecon Beacons** towards **Pontypool** along the **Usk Valley**, and then continues through a mixed rural and industrial landscape to **Newport**. It was built between 1797 and 1812, in an age when roads were notoriously bad, to carry limestone and processed lime from quarries at Trefil and Llangattock, which were linked to it by tramways.
www.waterscape.com

Nelson

Llancaiach Fawr Manor. Step back in time to 1645 and meet the servants of Colonel Pritchard, owner of this attractive house, as they recount tales about their lives. Listen to their gossip and hear about the customs of over three hundred and fifty years ago. A major topic will be the turmoil of the Civil War raging between King and Parliament. During the early part of the year there was staunch support for the Royalist cause but, following a visit by King Charles in August, the master and his household changed their allegiance in favour of the Parliamentarians.
• Follow signposted minor roads for Nelson and Llancaiach Fawr from the A470 north of Pontypridd and the A469 north of Caerphilly.
Phone: 01443 412248
www.caerphilly.gov.uk

New Tredegar

Elliot Colliery Winding House. The sight of the massive steam winding engine in action will bring home the scale of the activity and the danger of going underground. At its peak, Elliot Colliery, owned by the Powell Duffryn Steam Coal Company, employed around 2,800 people and produced over a million tons of high-quality steam coal each year.
• Some ten miles north of Caerphilly, off the A469.
Phone: 01443 822666
www.caerphilly.gov.uk

Pontypridd

Rhondda Heritage Park. The former Lewis Merthyr Colliery at Trehafod, at the gateway to the Rhondda valley, is now an entertaining and educational museum of coal mining. The looming presence of the pithead winding gear, surrounded by terraces of colliers' houses spreading up the hillsides, was once the defining feature of the densely populated mining towns that grew along the valleys from the mid-19th century onwards.
• Just west of Pontypridd on the A4058.
Phone: 01443 682036
www.rhonddaheritagepark.com

Right:
Llancaiach Fawr. Re-enactments of daily life are a popular attraction at this historic house. You can rely on the servants to spill the latest gossip about the master and his family!

Below:
Rhondda Heritage Park. One of the top heritage attractions in the Valleys, the Rhondda Heritage Park includes a multi-media exhibition, museum, art gallery and shop – as well as a tour to experience the working conditions in the Lewis Merthyr Colliery during the 1950s.

The Muni Arts Centre. In this beautiful converted church in the centre of Pontypridd, you can enjoy a programme of all kinds of music, exhibitions, dance, comedy, puppetry, productions by community groups, and events for children and young people. The venue also includes the Footlights Cafe Bar and the Gallery Shop.
• Programmes are available from the centre, local shops and library or via the Arts Council of Wales website.
Phone: 01443 485934
www.muniartscentre.co.uk

Tredegar

Sirhowy Ironworks. This site at Tredegar is a rare survivor of the early iron industry: the carefully conserved buildings date back to 1778. In 1818, the works were acquired by one James Harford of Ebbw Vale and began operating as a supplier to the Ebbw Vale Ironworks in the next valley to the east. Sirhowy provided pig iron that was worked into wrought iron and later, from the end of the 19th century, into steel.
• Five miles north-east of Merthyr Tydfil, take the Dukestown exit from the A4048 Tredegar bypass – past a petrol station and through a gap in the terrace of houses.
Phone: 01495 355537
www.blaenau-gwent.gov.uk

Treorchy

The Parc and Dare Theatre. This magnificent building, towering above the terraces of Treorchy, was built in 1913. It was funded by the workers of the Park and Dare collieries, who donated a penny for each pound of their wages so that they and their families could benefit from the cultural and educational opportunities provided by a miners' institute. It is home to the famous Treorchy male-voice choir, the multiple-prizewinning Parc and Dare Band and Rhondda Cynon Taff Community Arts. Top international musicians also grace the vigorous programme.
• This fine building towers over the terraces of Treorchy, in the Rhondda valley

north-west of Pontypridd, and is visible for miles around.
Phone: 01443 773112
www.rhondda-cynon-taff.gov.uk

Mining Valleys. The names of the mining towns – Porth, Tonypandy, Treorchy, Treherbert, Blaenrhondda, Maerdy, Ferndale, **Llwynypia** – resonate with the memory of the hard times endured by these close-knit communities. The memorial at Llwynypia, depicting a miner and his family, is especially moving.
www.rhondda-cynon-taff.gov.uk

Festivals and events

The Big Cheese. Set in the shadows of one of Europe's largest castles, Caerphilly Castle, The Big Cheese held in **July** is an extravaganza of street entertainers, living history encampments, music, dance and traditional funfair, portraying the history, heritage and culture of Caerphilly.
• www.caerphilly.gov.uk/visiting

The Big Balloon. Balloons of all shapes, sizes and colours gather at the Blackwood Showfields over the **August Bank Holiday** weekend for the Big Balloon Festival. The highlight of the weekend is the nightglow and fireworks display which takes place on the Sunday evening.
• www.caerphilly.gov.uk/visiting

Jazz in the Park. Jazz in the Park is held annually in **September** in the beautiful surroundings of Pontypool Park. The event includes international stars as well as local bands and attracts thousands of Jazz lovers.
• www.torfaenjazz.org

The Big Welsh Bite. Held in **August** at Pontypridd's Ynysangharad Memorial Park, The Big Welsh Bite is a food and agricultural event which takes as its theme 'Food and Agriculture through the Ages.' The weekend event has celebrity chef cooking demonstrations, animal displays and food and craft stalls.
• www.rhondda-cynon-taff.gov.uk

Cardiff and Vale of Glamorgan

Experience capital and countryside in harmony as you savour multicultural Cardiff, the Millennium Stadium, Castell Coch, Llandaff Cathedral, the Wales Millennium Centre, St Fagans National History Museum, St David's Hall, the Norwegian Church Cultural Centre and Cowbridge.

Above:
Cardiff. Few cities have so much green space, and such attractive civic buildings, as Cardiff – the Civic Centre is on the left and the castle is at lower right.

Above:
Civic Centre. The fine Portland stone buildings of Cardiff's Civic Centre have been compared to the similarly emphatic architectural expressions of civic pride to be found in Washington DC and New Delhi.

Barry

Cold Knap. This site dates from the latter days of the Roman presence in Wales during the 3rd and 4th centuries, and is believed to have been a small naval depot and coastal settlement served by a ferry. Nearby **Cold Knap Farm**, built in the 16th century, is the oldest house in Barry.
• From Barry's redeveloped waterfront, follow signs to Barry Island and Cold Knap. www.barrywales.co.uk

Barry. The town of Barry grew to prominence around the docks that David Davies of Llandinam built to serve his coal mines, in competition with the docks of Cardiff. Down at the redeveloped waterfront there is a fine statue of him studying the plans for his docks; an identical statue, far away from the sea, is sited in his home village.
www.barrywales.co.uk

Bridgend

Newcastle Hill. Now a conservation area, this oldest part of Bridgend is centred on the remains of the castle and the character-filled streets of cottages surrounding it. Amongst the older buildings is **St John's Hospice**, where weary pilgrims would rest on their way to **St David's** in Pembrokeshire. Leaflets are available for self-guided walks.
• Bridgend is accessible by J35/J36 of the M4.

Brynmenyn

Bryngarw House. A couple of miles north of Bridgend, you will find this fine country house with its smartly furnished rooms, standing in 113 acres of parkland. There is a visitor centre and exhibition, along with a children's play area and the Harlequin restaurant.
• North of Bridgend, a couple of miles from J36 of the M4 motorway.
Phone: 01656 729009
www.bridgend.gov.uk

Left:
Cardiff Castle.
At Cardiff Castle, visit the Norman Keep and the amazingly ornate home of the Bute family.

Cardiff

Cardiff Civic Centre. The majestic Portland stone buildings of the Civic Centre were designed as statements of civic pride by the Edwardian city fathers who steered Cardiff's development into the world's busiest coal port. **City Hall** – with its tall clock tower, graceful Renaissance embellishments and a dome topped by a fierce looking coiled dragon – was under construction when Cardiff gained city status in 1905. Upstairs, there are fine statues of famous figures from Welsh history. Other buildings in the group include the **Crown Courts**, the **National Museum Cardiff**, executive offices of the **National Assembly for Wales**, the **Temple of Peace** (home to the **Welsh Centre for International Affairs**) and several departments of **Cardiff University**.
• Cardiff's Civic Centre is prominent as you approach the city centre by road from the north.
www.cardiff.gov.uk

Multicultural Cardiff. The proportion of people whose families originated from elsewhere in the world is, as one would expect, greater in the seaport city of Cardiff than in other parts of Wales. The **Butetown Community and Arts Centre** tells the story of how the docklands of Tiger Bay became one of Britain's most cosmopolitan communities. The **MAS Carnival** brings the exuberance of the Caribbean and Rio de Janeiro to Cardiff Bay each summer. The world's major religions enjoy an atmosphere of mutual respect in the city. Cardiff's twelve mosques serve the large Muslim community, and Jewish, Afro-Caribbean, Chinese, Hindu, Sikh and Buddhist communities meet at their respective centres, invigorated by Cardiff's popularity with students from all parts of the globe.
• Butetown History and Arts Centre is in Bute Street, close to Cardiff Bay rail station.
Phone: 029 2025 6757
www.bhac.org

Cardiff Castle. Each phase of this marvellous site's evolution over the past two thousand years is accessible. The Romans established a fort here, the foundations of which have been incorporated into the castle's outer walls. The Normans showed who was boss by building the intimidating keep. In Tudor times, the Herbert family lived in style in their mansion. During the 1860s, the eccentric Victorian architect William Burges transformed the Third Marquess of Bute's home into one of the most extravagant examples of Gothic Revival fantasy to be found anywhere.
• Follow signs from the M4 to the city centre and convenient pay-and-display car parks.
Phone: 029 2087 8100
www.cardiffcastle.com

Welch Regiment Museum at Cardiff Castle. Displays of uniforms, weapons, medals and memorabilia commemorate the services of the Welch Regiment, which was founded in 1719 and absorbed into the Royal Regiment of Wales in 1969. The support given to the regular battalions by the Glamorgan militia and auxiliary land forces – including the Infantry, the Rifle Volunteers and the Yeomanry Cavalry – is recorded. The museum shop has a good range of books and regimental souvenirs.
• You may visit the museum, the main castle buildings and the grounds separately.
Phone: 029 2022 9367
www.rrw.org.uk

Llandaff Cathedral. Occupying a site that has been sacred since the 6th century, Llandaff Cathedral blends a Victorian structure with modern additions, including the sublime sculpture Christ in Majesty by Sir Jacob Epstein, and the Welch Regiment Memorial Chapel, dedicated to St David. In addition to being a place of worship, the cathedral also hosts concerts and exhibitions.
• Cardiff's Cathedral Road, across the River Taff from the castle, leads to Llandaff village.
Phone: 029 2056 4554
www.llandaffcathedral.org.uk

Left:
Millennium Stadium. Since opening in June 1999, this world-class venue has welcomed over 1.3 million visitors each year. It has the first retractable roof in the UK and is used for major sporting events and concerts.

Above:
Llandaff Cathedral. The striking interior of Llandaff Cathedral is an inspiring combination of restored Victorian Gothic and 20th-century styles.

Millennium Stadium. Located in the centre of Cardiff, this is the shrine of the national game, rugby football. Emotions run high when the team sprints out from the tunnel, to thunderous applause and cheering, to join in the national anthem and to be inspired to great feats of skill and bravery by the sound of tens of thousands of supporters singing the favourite hymns of their homeland. For many people, the cultural identity of Wales is inseparable from the game of rugby. For them, it is part of the heart and soul of the nation and – at least when the team is doing well – a source of national pride on a world stage.
• The Millennium Stadium and Cardiff Rugby Club are next door to each other, between the river and the city centre. Phone: 029 2082 2228 (stadium tours) www.millenniumstadium.com

City venues. As befits a capital city, Cardiff has a wealth of cultural venues to suit all tastes. The **Cardiff International Arena** can seat up to five thousand people and is the main venue for rock and pop music, and for the really big international stars. Cardiff-born Shirley Bassey has raised the roof there on numerous occasions. The **New Theatre**, a traditional Edwardian playhouse dating from 1906, puts on high-calibre drama, dance, musicals and pantomime. The **Sherman Theatre** nurtures tomorrow's talent by staging new plays and promoting youth projects. **Cardiff University's School of Music**, and the **Royal Welsh College of Music and Drama** present frequent public performances. **Chapter Arts Centre** serves up a diverse menu of film, theatre, dance and fine art. **The Gate** and **Llanover Hall** are community arts centres especially popular for their classes and workshops.
• Llanover Hall and Chapter Arts Centre are in Canton, across the river from the city centre. The Gate is in Roath.

St David's Hall. Conveniently situated at the heart of Cardiff's city centre, St David's Hall is the National Concert Hall of Wales. Its pleasant auditorium accommodates a

wide range of entertainment, including classical music, pop, rock, folk, jazz, world music, comedy, film and dance, along with exhibitions and conferences. World-class concerts feature the **BBC National Orchestra of Wales** as well as many famous visiting orchestras, chamber ensembles, soloists and conductors. The **Welsh Proms** concerts provide an uplifting celebration of classical music each summer. The biennial **BBC Cardiff Singer of the World** competition is a respected launch pad for future international stars of opera house and recital stage.
• Overlooking The Hayes, at the heart of Cardiff's shopping centre.
Phone: 029 2087 8444
www.stdavidshallcardiff.co.uk

National Museum Cardiff. In fascinating displays about history, science and art, this fine building houses vast collections of material including rocks, minerals and fossils; prehistoric and Celtic artefacts; five centuries' worth of paintings, sculpture and decorative art; and natural history specimens ranging from Snowdonia's delicate arctic-alpine plants to the skeleton of a whale. Highlights include superb Impressionist and Post-Impressionist paintings by Monet, Renoir, Cézanne, Van Gogh and others. These were given to the museum by the sisters Gwendoline and Margaret Davies, beneficiaries of the fortune derived from coal mines, railways and Barry Docks by their grandfather, David Davies of Llandinam. The international Artes Mundi visual-art competition is held at the museum in even-numbered years, when conceptual works of outstanding imagination are displayed. As with all National Museum Wales locations, admission is free.
• As you face the impressive Civic Centre, the National Museum Cardiff is the building to the right – **City Hall**, in the middle, is also worth a look, for its fine paintings and statues of historical figures.
Phone: 029 2039 7951
www.museumwales.ac.uk

Left and above:
Cardiff Bay.
Historic docklands have been transformed into a high-quality leisure, business and cultural environment.

Below:
Norwegian Church.
A dramatic statue of Captain Scott stands near this attractive cultural venue.

Cardiff Bay

Impressive listed buildings and preserved dockland fixtures lend historical integrity to the redeveloped waterfront of Cardiff Bay. During the second half of the 19th century, as a consequence of the coal-mining boom in the valleys to the north, Cardiff grew rapidly as a seaport and centre of commerce, and was granted city status in 1905. By 1913, this was the world's largest coal-exporting port, drawing in a cosmopolitan population that formed the foundation of today's vibrantly multicultural city.
• Prominently signed from J33 on the M4, and from the city centre.
www.cardiffbay.co.uk

Bay Art. In this modern gallery near the Wales Millennium Centre, you will find for sale a tremendous selection of high-quality contemporary art in many media. Regular exhibitions feature the best amongst established and emerging painters, sculptors, printers, ceramicists, jewellers and others. See programme for workshops, seminars and artist interviews.
• 54B/C Bute Street
Phone: 029 2065 0016
www.bayart.org.uk

Norwegian Church Cultural Centre. This picturesque former church was built to serve the spiritual needs of Norwegian seafarers whose ships brought in timber to make pit props for the coal mines inland. It is now a popular venue for music, literary events and exhibitions of painting and photography. Some of its events have Scandinavian themes and are organised in partnership with Cardiff's twin region of Hordaland in Norway. The author Roald Dahl was born in Cardiff in 1916 to Norwegian parents (his father was a shipbroker) and was baptised in this church.
• At Cardiff Bay's Inner Harbour, near the Wales Millennium Centre.
Phone: 029 2045 4899

Left and above: National Assembly for Wales. There is public access to much of the interior of the building – the transparency of the structure is intentionally symbolic of the openness of the work that goes on there, which you may view from the large public gallery.

Welsh Assembly Building. The sixty members of the National Assembly for Wales meet to discuss and vote upon policy in this striking building overlooking Cardiff Bay. In a gesture of faith that the National Assembly's powers might evolve further, the new building has been named the Senedd, the Welsh word for a senate or parliament. The circular Debating Chamber is intended to encourage the politicians to work in a constructive spirit of co-operation; their deliberations may be viewed from the public gallery above. Illuminated by daylight, the building is a showpiece of high-quality Welsh building materials including wood, steel and slate. The welcoming staff will quickly help you through the airport-style security system at the entrance and you are then free to explore the public areas, which include a café. The adjacent **Pierhead Building** houses the **National Assembly for Wales Visitor and Education Centre**, where you may learn how in many areas of life Wales is governed regionally, with decision-making devolved from Parliament in London.
• Near the **Wales Millennium Centre**, and close to train and bus services (for Cardiff Bay), a short walk from car parks at **Mermaid Quay** and the **Norwegian Church Cultural Centre**.
www.wales.gov.uk/assemblybuilding

Wales Millennium Centre. This landmark building at Cardiff Bay is one of the world's most innovative and dynamic performing arts venues, presenting a programme of entertainment that is second to none. The main Donald Gordon Theatre is a spectacular auditorium with acoustics and capabilities designed to delight performers and audiences alike. Innovative productions in the smaller studio theatre, daily events in the foyer and a selection of bars and restaurants make this a versatile must-see cultural destination. Seven organisations enjoy a synergetic neighbourliness at their bases here: **Welsh National Opera, Diversions Dance Company**, **Hijinx Theatre**, **Academi** (the literature promotion

Photograph Bill Cooper

Left:
Wales Millennium Centre. Composed by poet Gwyneth Lewis, the words above the entrance read: "Creu Gwir fel Gwydr o Ffwrnais Awen" – which means "Creating Truth like Glass from Inspiration's Furnace" – and "In these Stones Horizons Sing".

Above:
Magic Flute. This colourful production of The Magic Flute is one of many performances from the multi award-winning Welsh National Opera.

agency for Wales), **Touch Trust** (creative therapists), the **Tŷ Cerdd** music information centre and **Urdd Gobaith Cymru**, Wales's leading youth organisation.
• Signed from the city centre and accessible by train, taxi, public bus or Cardiff Tour bus.
Phone: 08700 402000
www.wmc.org.uk

Welsh National Opera. Wales is very fortunate to have its own world-class opera company – Welsh National Opera – which began as an amateur society some sixty years ago and now operates at the highest professional level from its state-of-the-art production base at the **Wales Millennium Centre.** Top international soloists and directors, a highly regarded orchestra and chorus, and skilled technical staff achieve exemplary standards. In addition to presenting a full programme of opera in Cardiff, from classical works to innovative modern productions, the company also goes on tour in the UK. A programme of community concerts, workshops and educational activities takes opera to local centres all over Wales.
Phone: 029 2063 5000
www.wno.org.uk

Cowbridge

There was a small town here in Roman times and today's High Street follows the Roman road Via Julia. The town walls and church were built in the 13th century, after which Cowbridge grew into its continuing role as a busy market town. The Grammar School was founded in 1608 and was owned between 1685 and 1918 by Jesus College, Oxford, which many of its pupils attended. Cowbridge is a prosperous, bustling place, famed for having the most upmarket high street of any town in Wales. Its restaurants, wine bars, antique shops and fashion boutiques occupy handsome 18th and 19th century houses and premises built for the merchants of this most attractive of towns.
www.cowbridge.co.uk

Left:
Cowbridge. The agreeable town of Cowbridge is a thoroughly pleasant place to explore – with its high-quality shops, attractive pubs and restaurants, and numerous historical sites.

Below:
Dyffryn Gardens. The Vale of Glamorgan is a haven of rural peace and Dyffryn Gardens is a special oasis of tranquillity where you will find formal gardens and open parkland that will revive the spirits in any season.

Plas Llanmihangel. This Elizabethan manor house has elements that date back to the 12th century. It is now operated as a guest house but there are guided tours for groups by arrangement, complemented by cream teas in the beautiful surroundings.
• A couple of miles south of Cowbridge along narrow country lanes.
Phone: 01446 774610

Llantwit Major

Llanilltyd Fawr. St Illtud founded a church, monastery and missionary centre here towards the end of the 5th century. This was one of the most important sites of the early Celtic church – a place of learning where both St David and St Patrick are believed to have been educated. Ancient Celtic crosses are to be seen in the church and around the churchyard.
• On the Glamorgan Heritage Coast, some five miles south of Cowbridge via the B4270.
www.llantwit-major.net

St Donat's. The medieval **St Donat's Castle** houses Atlantic College, the world's first international sixth-form college, where you may join guided tours during the holidays each August. The **St Donat's Arts Centre** is the Vale of Glamorgan's largest arts venue and offers a comprehensive programme in all genres.
• St Donat's is west of Llantwit Major: follow the B4270 from Cowbridge.
Phone: 01446 799000
www.atlanticcollege.org

Penarth

On the outskirts of Penarth, you will find the **Cosmeston Medieval Village** – a re-creation of a 14th century settlement where costumed guides will lead you into the past. Art lovers will find much of interest in the town. **The Turner House Art Gallery** displays fine paintings from the collections of the National Museum Wales. **The Oriel Washington Gallery** is housed in a striking Art Deco former cinema and displays an exciting selection of work for

sale by contemporary artists.
• The art galleries are close to the town centre. Cosmeston is south of Penarth, on the B4267.
www.valeofglamorgan.gov.uk

Penarth promenade and pier. The elegant Victorian town of Penarth has retained the appeal of its tranquil parks and gardens, its popular promenade and its ornate pier. Restaurants, ice cream parlours, gift shops and galleries pull in the crowds at weekends and holidays. The last seagoing paddle steamer, the Waverley, and the motor vessel Balmoral make numerous calls at the pier during the summer. In the tradition of the old Campbell's White Funnel steamers, they take passengers on cruises along the Welsh coast, around the islands of **Steep Holm** and **Flat Holm,** and across to Bristol, Somerset and Devon.
• Follow signs for Cardiff Bay and Penarth from J33 on the M4.
www.valeofglamorgan.gov.uk

Porthcawl

Porthcawl Grand Pavilion. This famous venue situated on the promenade is a seafront theatre offering a great programme of shows and concerts.
• South from J37 on the M4, via the A4229.
Phone: 01656 786996
www.bridgend.gov.uk

St Fagans

St Fagans National History Museum.
Here at one of the world's most impressive open-air museums, you will find more than forty buildings, ranging from a re-created **Celtic village** of two thousand years ago to the eco-friendly **House for the Future.** In beautiful parkland surrounding **St Fagans Castle,** authentic buildings – including farmhouses, barns, workers' cottages, village shops, a miners' institute, a woollen mill, a chapel and a church – have been transported stone by stone from all over Wales and meticulously rebuilt. The indoor galleries illuminate the social and cultural life of Wales through artefacts and costumes. Craft demonstrators around the site explain their skills as you watch. Events include celebrations at May Day and Christmas.
• Just south of J33 on the M4, regular bus services to St Fagans village.
Phone: 029 2057 3500
www.museumwales.ac.uk

St Nicholas

Dyffryn Gardens. These Grade I listed Edwardian landscaped gardens are among the largest and finest in Wales. Located between Cowbridge and Cardiff, they are a popular location for open-air concerts and theatre productions.
• Just south of St Nicholas, on the A48 west of Cardiff.
Phone: 029 2059 3328
www.dyffryngardens.org.uk

Taff's Well

Just north of Cardiff, the hot spring that gave its name to the village that grew around it has been known for its healing properties since Roman times. It has been neglected for many years but there are plans to restore it to use. Analysis of the water has shown it to have a similar mineral content to the springs at Bath.
• From J32 on the M4, the A470's busy junctions and sliproads lead to Taff's Well.
www.rhondda-cynon-taff.gov.uk

Above and right: **National History Museum.** The many attractions of this special place include traditional dancing on May Day, restored houses from all over Wales, the gardens and interiors of St Fagans Castle, educational activities for adults and children, and the atmospheric Gwalia Supply Company store.

Left and above: **Castell Coch.** A magical sight from the M4 just north of Cardiff, Castell Coch gives a convincing impression of a medieval fantasy castle. William Burges was able to let his imagination run riot, with no concern about cost, when he designed the astonishing rooms at Castell Coch.

Tongwynlais

The eccentric Victorian architect William Burges designed **Castell Coch** as a retreat for the Third Marquess of Bute and his family, though they spent little time here. Burges was inspired by chateaux in Switzerland and France to build an idealised reconstruction of the medieval castle of Gilbert the Red, Earl of Gloucester, which originally stood on this elevated site overlooking the Taff gorge at Tongwynlais. The exuberant interior is decorated with a riot of symbolic imagery derived from Classical mythology, Aesop's fables and medieval manuscripts, along with an eclectic assemblage of French, Gothic and Moorish influences.
• At Tongwynlais, within sight of J32 of the M4.
Phone: 029 2081 0101
www.cadw.wales.gov.uk

Vale of Glamorgan

The north-western part of the Vale of Glamorgan region extends towards the Valleys and includes the town of Maesteg and the upper part of the Ogmore valley. **Maesteg Town Hall** is a splendidly old-fashioned and homely building where you can enjoy concerts, drama and exhibitions. The **Blaengarw Workmen's Hall**, at the top of the Garw valley, is a cinema, theatre and dance venue. The **Berwyn Centre** at Nant y Moel is a theatre and exhibition centre.
• Head northward from J36 on the M4 to this region of industry and vigorous culture.

Festivals and events

Festivals. The **Cardiff Festival** is said to be Europe's biggest free festival, attracting upwards of five hundred thousand people to arts, music, theatre and comedy events at venues throughout the city, including its parks and streets. The **International Festival of Musical Theatre** is held every

Left:
WNO concert.
Cardiff Bay hosts open-air concerts by big names: this is Welsh National Opera.

Above:
Cardiff Festival.
At the heart of the Cardiff Festival is the very best of street theatre, live music, youth and children's entertainment, funfairs, food and drama. The Festival finishes with The Big Weekend – a three-day event with live outdoor music and funfair.

two years, alternating with **Cardiff Singer of the World**, and brings the best of musical theatre to the **Wales Millennium Centre**, the **New Theatre** and other venues. Down around the waterfront, the **Worldport Festival** celebrates Cardiff's role as a seaport by inviting world music performers to historic venues including **The Coal Exchange** – where many deals were agreed during the coal port's heyday – and **The Point**, a former church. **Gŵyl Ifan**, the UK's biggest folk-dancing festival, brings dance groups from the Celtic nations to Cardiff's city centre each June.
www.cardiff-festival.com

The **St Donat's Music Festival**, early each **September**, is a celebration of music by living composers.
• St Donat's is west of Llantwit Major: follow the B4270 from Cowbridge.
Phone: 01446 799000
www.atlanticcollege.org

Cardiff International Food & Drink Festival.
A key ingredient of the Cardiff Festival, the Cardiff International Food & Drink Festival, held in **July**, is a free food-lovers' paradise promoting the very finest in food, drink and entertainment from Wales and elsewhere, held at Roald Dahl's Plass, just in front of the Wales Millennium Centre.
Phone: 029 2087 2087
www.cardiff-festival.com

Heritage Weekend. The Heritage Weekend is held every **September** at Cosmeston Medieval Village, near Penarth. The buildings and costumed demonstrators recreate the year 1350, a troubled time in relations between Wales and England. Events include re-enactments, storytelling and archery.
• Cosmeston Medieval Village also organise events throughout the year – check with the local Tourist Information Centre for events and dates.
Phone: 029 2070 1678

Wye Valley and Vale of Usk

Follow Turner and Wordsworth to these vales of heritage and see Tintern Abbey, Offa's Dyke, the Monmouthshire and Brecon Canal, Abergavenny, Monmouth, Tredegar House, the National Roman Legion Museum, Usk Rural Life Museum, Llantilio Crossenny Festival and the Newport Riverfront Theatre.

Above:
Caerleon Roman Amphitheatre. Excavations at Caerleon's amphitheatre, barracks and baths have revealed valuable insights into the Roman occupation of Britain two millennia ago. There are authentic re-enactments here, each summer, of Roman military tactics.

Abergavenny

With a centre full of character reflecting its origins as a medieval market town, Abergavenny is an attractive place to explore. The **Abergavenny Museum**, housed in a hunting lodge within the walls of the castle, has reconstructions of a Victorian kitchen, a saddler's workshop and a 1950s grocery store.
• Well connected to the M4 and M50/M5 by the A40 and A449 dual carriageways. www.abergavenny.co.uk

Caerleon

Known to the Romans as Isca, this is one of the most revealing of their settlements to have been excavated anywhere in Europe. They built a large military base here, with barracks for the 5,500 members of the Second Augustan Legion. The adjacent township had an amphitheatre and a bath house – a leisure centre, in effect, with open-air swimming pool, covered exercise hall and a series of hot, warm and cold baths.

The historical significance of Caerleon, one of the three principal military bases of Roman Britannia, is reflected at the Roman Legionary Museum. Here you will find a reconstruction of a barrack room and fascinating displays of decorative art, weapons, domestic artefacts and architectural fragments, and even some gemstones lost by customers at the baths.

Also in Caerleon, the sculpture trail is a permanent legacy of the **International Sculpture and Arts Festival**, held each July, and the **Ffwrwm Art and Crafts Centre** is well worth a visit.
• Brown signs on the M4 point to this site of European importance just north of Newport. www.caerleon.net

Caerwent

This was the Roman provincial capital, Venta Silurum, and the first town in Wales.

Left:
Offa's Dyke. This is the linear earthwork that approximately marks the boundary between England and Wales. It consists of a ditch and rampart. As originally constructed, it must have been about 27 metres wide and 8 metres from the ditch bottom to the bank top.

Below:
Llanthony Priory. Go carefully along the narrow roads that lead to Llanthony Priory, in its serene surroundings.

It was founded in 75 AD after the territory of the local Silurian people was brought under control. Its street grid and amenities, including a basilica, forum, bath houses, shops and temples, evolved over the following three hundred years of Roman occupation. The town walls, up to sixteen feet (5m) high, remain impressive. At the height of its prosperity, the population of Venta Silurum, which means Market of the Silures, was probably around 2,500 – far greater than any other place in Wales would reach for some fifteen hundred years.
• Take the A48 from J24 of the M4, or from J2 on the M48, then left at the approach to Chepstow.

Chepstow

Chepstow Castle. The solid castle and remnants of the town walls underline Chepstow's importance as a strategic frontier settlement. **Chepstow Museum**, situated in an elegant 18th century house, covers the town's history as a port and market centre. There are displays on the wine trade, boatbuilding and salmon fishing. **St Mary's Church Walk** is a charming old street of quaint architecture and small shops; look out for the Art on the Railings events each summer.
• Reached via the M48 and the original Severn Bridge, not the M4 – or by the scenic Wye valley from Monmouth.
Phone: 01291 624065
www.cadw.wales.gov.uk

Offa's Dyke. King Offa of Mercia ordered the building of this earthwork not so much as a means of defence but as a line of demarcation between his territory and the vigorously defended kingdoms and princedoms of Wales to the west, which the Saxons never conquered. It has stood since the 8th century, and for much of its 182-mile length continues to be visible close to the border between Wales and England. The **Offa's Dyke Path National Trail** may be followed all the way from the estuary of the River Wye, near Chepstow, to Prestatyn on the north Wales coast.

• Maps and guidebooks are available from the Tourist Information Centre near Chepstow Castle.
www.offasdyke.demon.co.uk

Border castles. William Fitz Osbern, a supporter of William the Conqueror, started work on **Chepstow Castle** soon after 1066 to guard the strategic crossing point over the River Wye. The Normans soon consolidated their occupation of this corner of Wales. The numerous castles of this region, including **Abergavenny, Caldicot, Grosmont, Skenfrith, White Castle, Monmouth, Usk, Penhow and Raglan**, tell a story of increasingly stable and peaceful times as intimidating fortresses were superseded by the precursors of more comfortable country houses.
• Minor roads (B4347, B4233, B4521) north-west of Monmouth lead to Skenfrith, Grosmont and White Castle.
www.cadw.wales.gov.uk

Goytre Wharf

Call at this informative visitor centre on the **Monmouthshire and Brecon Canal** to learn how this scenic waterway was built to link Brecon and Newport. Tramways gave access from it to nearby quarries and to the ironworks of Blaenavon. Transportation by canal barge was the most efficient way of taking limestone and processed lime down to the docks at Newport, for export to other parts of Britain or overseas.
• Near Llanover, off the A4042 – there are scenic stretches of canal between here and Abergavenny.
Phone: 01873 881069
www.waterscape.com

Llanthony

Llanthony Priory. It was here that St David embarked upon his ascetic life as a hermit – drinking only water and eating only the wild leeks that would, as a consequence, become the emblem of Wales. The Priory, founded for Augustinian canons in 1107,

is a haven of tranquillity amid wondrous scenery. The church is aligned with the position on the ridge where the sun rises on St David's day, the 1st of March.
• From the A465, north of Abergavenny, follow narrow roads from Llanfihangel Crucorney.
www.cadw.wales.gov.uk

Skirrid Fawr. This distinctively shaped peak near Abergavenny has been considered a holy mountain for centuries: the Archangel Michael is said to have appeared here and there are remains of a sacred building on the cleft summit. This is where, during the Protestant Reformation, persecuted Catholics would meet in secret to celebrate Mass, at great risk to their lives.
• There are marked footpaths from the A465 and B4521 north of Abergavenny.
www.abergavenny.co.uk

Monmouth

Two fine statues overlook Monmouth's **Agincourt Square**. Henry V secured victory at that crucial battle through the services of archers from this part of the Welsh Borders. Charles Stewart Rolls, descended from a Monmouthshire family, teamed up with Henry Royce to found the famous manufacturers of aircraft engines and cars. Also in Monmouth, the hilltop site of The Kymin encompasses a circular two-storey banqueting house and a small temple dedicated to the glories of the Royal Navy; Nelson visited it in 1802. As is the case in so many historic towns throughout Wales, Monmouth makes the most of its cultural attributes. The **Nelson Museum** has one of the world's best collections of material relating to the legendary Admiral. The centrally located **Local History Museum**, **Monmouth Castle**, the **Regimental Museum** and the **Wyastone Leys Concert Hall**, just up the A499 from the town, contribute to the mix.
• www.monmouth.org.uk

Newport

The city of Newport stands at the mouth of the Usk, where it grew as a port serving the eastern valleys of the south Wales coalfield. Its **Transporter Bridge**, opened in 1906, is a triumph of engineering. People and cars are carried over in a gondola suspended beneath a structure tall enough for ships to pass beneath.

The City of Newport is rich in cultural attractions. The **Riverfront Theatre and Arts Centre**, just along the bank of the Usk from the ruins of the castle, is a superbly equipped modern theatre presenting a wealth of entertainment. The medieval ship uncovered when its foundations were dug, and the bones of an Iron Age man found below the ship, are being conserved for display. **Newport Museum and Art Gallery** exhibits material from Roman Caerwent and chronicles the Chartist Uprising. Just north of Newport, where a flight of locks raises the **Monmouthshire and Brecon Canal** 168 feet (51m) in half a mile (0.8km), the **Fourteen Locks Canal Centre** illustrates the growth and decline of water transport, and the industries it served since 1796.
• The city of Newport is mid-way between Cardiff and the Second Severn Crossing.
www.newport.gov.uk

St Woolo's Cathedral. Overlooking Newport from its hilltop site, this is the cathedral of the diocese of Monmouth. Its rather curious name is a corruption of Gwynllyw, the Welsh name of the 5th century saint who first ministered here. The Most Reverend Dr Rowan Williams served here as Bishop of Monmouth and Archbishop of Wales, before becoming Archbishop of Canterbury.
• The cathedral is a short drive or a moderate walk from Newport's city centre.
www.newport.gov.uk

WAY IN

TINTERN

Great Western Railway
RACES
CARDIFF

Above left:
Tredegar House.
This symmetrical
gem of Restoration
architecture is
attractively set
in fine parkland.

Above:
The Old Station.
Now incorporates
a café, miniature
railway and
exhibition room.

Left:
Tintern Abbey.
Located in an
official Area of
Outstanding Natural
Beauty, the abbey
has attracted
tourists since
Victorian times.

Tredegar House. Set in ninety acres of gardens and parkland, this outstanding example of Restoration architecture was the ancestral home of the Morgan family for more than five hundred years. Discover what life was like, both above and below stairs, as you tour the magnificent staterooms decorated with ornate carving, gilding and fine paintings, and the fascinating domestic quarters. The stable blocks house some excellent craft shops.
• Tredegar House is close to J28 on the M4, just west of Newport.
Phone: 01633 815880
www.newport.gov.uk

Tintern

The ruins of the magnificent Cistercian abbey of Tintern, founded in 1131, stand in a place of sublime beauty where the River Wye cuts through a narrow limestone gorge overlooked by 600-foot cliffs. The roof is gone and the interior is bare, but it

is still possible to imagine how this place of worship and contemplation must have looked before it was destroyed at the behest of Henry VIII.

A profoundly atmospheric place, Tintern inspired both JMW Turner and William Wordsworth. Today, it is the location of occasional son-et-lumiere performances and an annual candlelit carol service.
• Five miles north of Chepstow on the A466.
www.cadw.wales.gov.uk

Tintern Parva. The little village next to the abbey extends along the bank of the Wye and is the focal point of numerous well-signed footpaths. **The Abbey Mill**, a water mill once operated by the monks, houses an arts and crafts centre, a gift shop and a café. **The Old Station** just up the valley is a preserved Victorian country railway station with a signal box, and is a great spot for a picnic.
• Just north of the abbey; the village has grown along the river bank.
www.tintern.org.uk

Left:
Wye Valley. This Area of Outstanding Natural Beauty is a protected landscape surrounding a 72-mile stretch of the meandering river Wye between Chepstow and Hereford, along the border between England and Wales.

Above:
Cwmyoy Church. The walls and tower of Cwmyoy's remarkable church really do lean more than seems possible.

Trellech

Ancient standing stones, known in English as Harold's Stones, give their name to this village: in Welsh, tre-llech means three stones or slates. In medieval times, this was a substantial town and the area has many sites of historic interest. Terret Tump is a forty-foot (12m) high mound of earth that was once the motte for one of the many small wooden castles built hurriedly by the Normans. Trellech's holy well – St Anne's Well, or the Virtuous Well – used to be a place of pilgrimage. The churchyard contains a large pedestal, once the foundation for an ancient cross.
• Take the B4293 northward from Chepstow or southward from Monmouth.
www.wyenot.com/trellech.htm

Usk

Usk Rural Life Museum. Crammed with reminders of the region's rural heritage, this museum occupies the old **Malt Barn** in the attractive town of Usk. Follow the countryman's year as you see local wagons, vintage machinery and reconstructions of a farmhouse kitchen, laundry and dairy – and much more.
• The small town of Usk is just off the A449 north of Newport.
Phone. 01291 673777

Wye Valley

Churches. Ancient churches abound in Monmouthshire, many of them in remote places. **St Martin's Church** at Cwmyoy stands on land that has subsided and no parts of its walls and tower seem to be square with any other. **Patrishow Church** is distinguished by a remarkable rood screen and loft dating from around 1500, a font bearing an inscription from around 1055, and a series of wall paintings. **Penallt Old Church** commands glorious views of the Wye valley.
• Cwmyoy and Patrishow are off the A465 north of Abergavenny; Penallt is just south of Monmouth, off the A466 or B4293.

Above, above left and far left:
Abergavenny Food Festival. High-quality Welsh ingredients are celebrated, cooked, eaten and sold at the Abergavenny Food Festival.

Left:
Living history. Look out for authentic re-enactments at castles and historic houses.

Festivals and events

Abergavenny Food Festival. The liveliest, most cultured and quirkiest food festival in the UK, the Abergavenny Food Festival is held every **September** and celebrates the best of Welsh and British food. A must-visit for any food lover, the festival is held at numerous venues and streets in the town. Activities include cheese and wine tasting, chef's demos, and talks, as well as food stalls galore and a full programme of events.
Phone: 01873 851643
www.abergavennyfoodfestival.com

Cultural festivals. For ten days each summer, the **Abergavenny Festival** brings a wide range of musical, dramatic, literary and visually artistic activity to the picturesque town. The **Tredegar House Folk Festival**, held every **May**, sees dancers and musicians performing in traditional styles. The **Monmouth Festival** brings a wide choice of performances and exhibitions to the town during early August.

Llantilio Crossenny Festival of Music and Drama. This small village between Abergavenny and Monmouth is home to a high quality festival of classical music, opera and ballet, which has been held at **St Teilo's Church** each **May** for more than forty years.
• Mid-way between Abergavenny and Monmouth, on the B4233.
Phone: 01873 856928
www.llantiliocrossenny.com

History brought to life. The castles and historic houses of this south-eastern corner of Wales provide authentic locations for battle re-enactments and more gentle historically themed entertainments. Look out for military spectaculars, medieval days, son-et-lumiere displays, concerts and open-air theatre performances at the likes of **Caldicot**, **Usk**, **Abergavenny** and **Chepstow Castles** and the **Caerleon Roman amphitheatre**.
• Tourist Information Centres have dates and details of historical re-enactments.

Where to eat and stay

Alphabetical listing by region with contact details of restaurants and accommodation

North Wales

Bistro Conwy, Conwy
Phone: 01492 596326
www.bistroconwy.com

Bodysgallen Hall*, Llandudno
Phone: 01492 584466
www.bodysgallen.com

Brasserie, Ye Olde Bull's Head*,
Beaumaris
Phone: 01248 810329
www.bullsheadinn.co.uk

Bryn Tyrch*, Betws-y-coed
Phone: 01690 720223
www.bryntyrch-hotel.co.uk

Castle Cottage*, Harlech
Phone: 01766 780479
www.castlecottageharlech.co.uk

Castle Hotel, Shakespeares Restaurant*, Conwy
Phone: 01492 582800
www.castlewales.co.uk

Granvilles, Criccieth
Phone: 01766 522506

Le Gallois, Penmaenmawr
Phone: 01492 623820

Lobster Pot*, Nr Holyhead
Phone: 01407 730241
www.thelobsterpot.info

Maes-y-Neuadd*, Talsarnau
Phone: 01766 780200
www.neuadd.com

Penhelig Arms*, Aberdovey
Phone: 01654 767215
www.penheligarms.com

Plas Bodegroes*, Pwllheli
Phone: 01758 612363
www.bodegroes.co.uk

Porth Tocyn Hotel*, Abersoch
Phone: 01758 713303
www.porth-tocyn-hotel. co.uk

Portmeirion Hotel*, Portmeirion
Phone: 01766 770000
www.portmeirion-village.com

Queen's Head*, Nr Penrhyn Bay
Phone: 01492 546570

Stables Bar Restaurant, Mold
Phone: 01352 840577
www.soughtonhall.co.uk

St Tudno Hotel*, Llandudno
Phone: 01492 874411
www.st-tudno.co.uk

Tan-y-Foel*, Nr Betws-y-coed
Phone: 01690 710507
www.tyfhotel.co.uk

Trearddur Bay Hotel*, Nr Holyhead
Phone: 01407 860301
www.trearddurbayhotel.co.uk

Tyddyn Llan*, Nr Corwen
Phone: 01490 440264
www.tyddynllan.co.uk

Waterfront, Nr Holyhead
Phone: 01407 860006

Mid Wales

Bear Hotel*, Crickhowell
Phone: 01873 810408
www.bearhotel.co.uk

Carlton House*, Llanwrtyd Wells
Phone: 01591 610248
www.carltonrestaurant.co.uk

Conrah*, Nr Aberystwyth
Phone: 01970 617941
www.conrah.co.uk

Harbourmaster*, Aberaeron
Phone: 01545 570755
www.harbour-master.com

Hive on the Quay, Aberaeron
Phone: 01545 570445
www.hiveonthequay.co.uk

Lake Country House*,
Llangammarch Wells
Phone: 01591 620202
www.lakecountryhouse.co.uk

Lake Vyrnwy Hotel*, Llanwddyn
Phone: 01691 870692
www.lakevyrnwy.com

Llangoed Hall*, Llyswen
Phone: 01874 754525
www.llangoedhall.com

Nantyffin Cider Mill, Crickhowell
Phone: 01873 810775
www.cidermill.co.uk

Milebrook House*, Knighton
Phone: 01547 528632
www.milebrookhouse.co.uk

Penbontbren*, Nr Cardigan
Phone: 01239 810248
www.penbontbren.com

Seeds, Llanfyllin
Phone: 01691 648604

Talkhouse*, Pontdolgoch
Phone: 01686 688919
www.talkhouse.co.uk

Tipple 'n' Tiffin, Brecon
Phone: 01874 611866

Waterdine*, Llanfair
Phone: 01547 528214
www.waterdine.com

West Arms*, Nr Llangollen
Phone: 01691 600665
www.thewestarms.co.uk

Wynnstay*, Machynlleth
Phone: 01654 702941
www.wynnstay-hotel.com

Ynyshir Hall*, Nr Machynlleth
Phone: 01654 781209
www.ynyshir-hall.co.uk

South west Wales

Angel Inn, Salem
Phone: 01558 823394

Butchers Arms, Llanddarog
Phone: 01267 275330

Cnapan*, Newport
Phone: 01239 820575
www.online-holidays.net/ cnapan

Cors*, Laugharne
Phone: 01994 427219

Didier & Stephanie's, Swansea
Phone: 01792 655603

Druidstone*, Haverfordwest
Phone: 01437 781221
www.druidstone.co.uk

Fairyhill*, Gower
Phone: 01792 390139
www.fairyhill.net

Falcon*, Carmarthen
Phone: 01267 237152
www.falconcarmarthen.co.uk

Hanson's, Swansea
Phone: 01792 466200

Hurst House*, Laugharne
Phone: 01994 427417
www.hurst-house.co.uk

King Arthur, Reynoldston
Phone: 01792 390775
www.kingarthurhotel.co.uk

Knights, Mumbles
Phone: 01792 363184

La Braseria, Swansea
Phone: 01792 469683
www.labraseria.com

Lower Haythog Farm*,
Nr Haverfordwest
Phone: 01437 731279
www.lowerhaythogfarm.co.uk

Old Kings Arms*, Pembroke
Phone: 01646 683611
www.oldkingsarmshotel.co.uk

PA's Wine Bar, Mumbles
Phone: 01792 367723
www.paswinebar.co.uk

St Brides*, Saundersfoot
Phone: 01834 812304
www.stbrideshotel.com

Stone Hall*, Nr Haverfordwest
Phone: 01348 840212
www.stonehall-mansion. co.uk

Tregynon Farmhouse*,
Nr Fishguard
Phone: 07970 627910
www.tregynon-cottages.co.uk

Welcome to Town Inn, Llanrhidian
Phone: 01792 390015
www.thewelcometotown.co.uk

Yr Hen Dafarn, Llansteffan
Phone: 01267 241656

South east Wales

Armless Dragon, Cardiff
Phone: 029 2038 2357
www.armlessdragon.co.uk

Bell at Skenfrith*, Skenfrith
Phone: 01600 750235
www.skenfrith.com

Clytha Arms*, Nr Abergavenny
Phone: 01873 840206
www.clytha-arms.com

Da Venditto, Cardiff
Phone: 029 2023 0781
www.vendittogroup.co.uk

Felin Fach Griffin*, Felin Fach
Phone: 01874 620111
www.eatdrinksleep.ltd.uk

Foxhunter, Nant-y-Derry
Phone: 01873 881101
www.thefoxhunter.com

Frolics, Southerndown
Phone: 01656 880127

Le Gallois – Y Cymro, Cardiff
Phone: 029 2034 1264
www.legallois-ycymro.com

Old Post Office*, Cardiff
Phone: 029 2056 5400
www.old-post-office.com

Owens*, Newport
Phone: 01633 410262
www.celtic-manor.com

Walnut Tree, Nr Abergavenny
Phone: 01873 852797
www.thewalnuttreeinn.com

Woods Brasserie, Cardiff
Phone: 029 2049 2400
www.woods-brasserie.com

*Accommodation available

Information and useful websites

Tourist Information Centres throughout Wales have expert and welcoming staff who can offer independent assistance with planning routes, booking accommodation and the search for information on places or events to visit. They are your one stop-shop for holiday and short break information, late availability and last minute offers.

For a full list of Tourist Information Centres www.visitwales.com

Tourist Information Centres:
The Isle of Anglesey
T 01248 713177
Snowdonia Mountains and Coast/Eryri Mynyddoedd a Môr
T 01690 710426
Llandudno, Colwyn Bay, Rhyl and Prestatyn T 01492 876413
The North Wales Borderlands
T 01978 860828
Mid Wales and the Brecon Beacons
T 01686 625580
Ceredigion – Cardigan Bay
T 01970 612125
Pembrokeshire T 01834 842402
Carmarthenshire – the Garden of Wales T 01267 231557

Swansea Bay – the Gower Peninsula, Mumbles, Afan and the Vale of Neath T 01792 468321
Wisdom and Walks in the Valleys of south Wales T 029 2088 0011
Cardiff T 029 2022 7281
The Glamorgan Heritage Coast and Countryside T 01656 654906
Wye Valley and Vale of Usk
T 01291 623772

Useful websites

Castles and heritage:
www.cadw.wales.gov.uk
www.nationaltrust.org.uk
www.bbc.co.uk/wales/history
(BBC Wales)
www.llgc.org.uk (National Library of Wales)
www.kingarthurslabyrinth.com
www.merlinshill.com
www.cardiff.gov.uk/castle
(Cardiff Castle)
www.dylanthomas.org
www.gardenofwales.org.uk
(National Botanic Garden)
www.aberglasney.org
www.bodnantgarden.co.uk

Museums and galleries:
www.museumwales.ac.uk
www.waterfrontmuseum.co.uk
www.cymal.wales.gov.uk/museum/index (national and local museums)
www.bodelwyddan-castle.co.uk
(including National Portrait Gallery)

Festivals and events:
www.eisteddfod.org.uk
(the National Eisteddfod of Wales)
www.international-eisteddfod.co.uk
(Llangollen Eisteddfod)
www.urdd.org (Urdd Youth Eisteddfod)
www.brynfest.com
(Bryn Terfel's Faenol Festival)

www.artswales.org.uk
(Arts Council of Wales)
www.cerddystwyth.co.uk (festivals list by Aberystwyth music shop)
www.victorianfestival.co.uk
(Llandrindod Wells)
www.hayfestival.co.uk
(Hay Festival of Literature)
www.rwas.co.uk
(Royal Welsh Show)
www.breconjazz.co.uk
(Brecon Jazz Festival)
www.cardiffmusicals.com
(Festival of Musical Theatre)
www.thingstodo.org.uk
www.llanwrtyd-wells.powys.org.uk
www.homecomingwales.com
(choir listings)
www.cardiff-festival.com
www.millenniumstadium.com
www.wmc.org.uk
(Wales Millennium Centre)
www.wno.org.uk
(Welsh National Opera)

Websites
www.city-sightseeing.com
(Cardiff bus tours)
www.portmeirion-village.com
www.ccw.gov.uk (National Trails)
www.snowdonia-npa.gov.uk
(Snowdonia National Park)
www.pembrokeshirecoast.org
(Pembrokeshire Coast National Park)
www.visitbreconbeacons.org
(Brecon Beacons National Park)

How to get here

By car. The UK's road network serves visitors to Wales well, making it easy to get to by car. You can get to south Wales along the M4 and on to west Wales along the connecting dual carriageway system. In the north the A55 coastal Expressway provides a trouble-free, fast route to the north coast, while the M54 connects mid Wales to the M6 and beyond.

By train. Wales is easy to get to from all of the UK. From London Paddington there is a frequent express service that will take you to Cardiff in only two hours. It also takes around two hours to get from Manchester to the resort of Llandudno on Wales's north coast. If you are visiting from overseas you will find that there are good links between all major airports and the main rail network. For rail enquiries and booking ring + 44(0) 8457 48 49 50 or visit one of the following websites: www.nationalrail.co.uk, www.thetrainline.com or www.qjump.co.uk

By coach or bus. National Express offers a nationwide service of fast, reliable express coaches. There is a good service from London Victoria coach station to many towns and cities in Wales as well as from many cities and towns in both England and Scotland. For example, the journey time between London and Newport is around three hours. There are also convenient Flightlink coach services from major airports to destinations in Wales. For information and bookings call + 44 (0) 8705 808080 or go to:

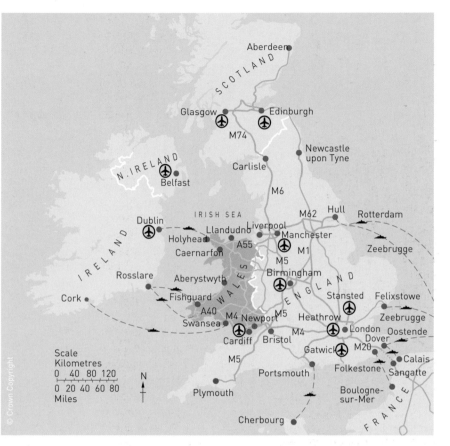

www.nationalexpress.co.uk
Inside Wales there is an extensive network of regional and local bus services.

By air. There are regular direct flights to Cardiff International Airport from a wide range of destinations, including Amsterdam, Cork, Glasgow, London City, Paris and Prague. Also, Amsterdam, Dublin and Paris act as gateway hubs for European and international flights. For flight information call +44 (0) 1446 711111 email infodesk@cwl.aero or visit www.cial.co.uk
London's airports and those at Birmingham and Manchester are all good gateways to Wales. Each has good road and rail connections.

By sea. Three ferry companies operate services between Wales and Ireland. They are:
Irish Ferries. Dublin to Holyhead, and Rosslare to Pembroke
Tel: +44 (0) 8705 171717
www.irishferries.com
Stena Line. Dun Laoghaire or Dublin to Holyhead, and Rosslare to Fishguard
Tel: +44 (0) 8705 707070
www.stenaline.co.uk
Swansea-Cork Ferries
Cork to Swansea
Tel: +44 (0) 1792 456116
www.swansea-cork.ie

The Welsh language

The ancient language of Wales is very much alive during the 21st century and is spoken by around half a million people.

It is a fully functioning modern language, taught in schools and studied in universities, through which all aspects of social and business life may be conducted. It contributes to the distinctiveness of Wales amongst the other nations of the United Kingdom.

Welsh evolved from the Celtic languages spoken throughout Britain at the time of the Roman occupation. These included two distinct forms: the Goidelic group, which produced the Irish, Scots Gaelic and Manx (Isle of Man) languages, and the Brythonic group, from which the Welsh, Cornish and Breton languages emerged.

Welsh is one of Europe's oldest languages and is by far the strongest survivor of all the Celtic tongues. As with all languages, it has over many centuries absorbed words and influences from elsewhere, since its forced encounter with Latin onwards. Geographical differences in dialect remain – between northern, southern, western and border regions of Wales – but the unifying influences of education, improved travel links, publishing and broadcasting mean that these have diminished and may be now regarded as interesting aspects of a rich tapestry, rather than as obstacles to communication.

Welsh is seen and heard throughout Wales. It is especially strong in the more rural areas of the north and west but there are also some 30,000 fluent speakers in Cardiff, many of whom work in education, public administration or the media. The

1993 Welsh Language Act states that all public sector bodies must give equal status to Welsh and English, and enshrines the right to use the Welsh language in a court of law.

The Welsh Language Board advises the public sector and the world of business on Welsh language usage, contributes to Welsh-language education, including classes for learners, and maintains a database of qualified translators. At the most detailed level, it also participates in the devising of new words, including technical, scientific and popular culture terms.

Welsh and English are the official languages of government, with documents available in both. In the debating chamber of the National Assembly for Wales, members are free to speak in whichever language they choose, and impressively quick-thinking simultaneous translators, with the necessary technical vocabulary, relay the proceedings to all other members and to the public gallery.

The language is taught as part of the National Curriculum in schools throughout Wales, up to age sixteen. Growing numbers of pupils from both Welsh-speaking and non-Welsh-speaking families are being educated in Welsh medium schools, which have attained high educational standards.

The substantial Welsh-language output of S4C, the fourth television channel, which is available both terrestrially and digitally, has further boosted the language. The BBC has long been a pillar of Welsh-language culture, producing television and radio programmes, including educational ones, and broadcasting cultural events. BBC Radio Cymru is broadcast nationally and also reaches Welsh people in much of England, as well as being available to Welsh expatriates all over the world via the internet.

If you don't have the language yourself, you will find that Wales is a bilingual country and that everyone speaks English. It is also a multicultural country where numerous other languages are in use, especially in the cities, by people drawn here from overseas. Over the previous century and more, people arrived from elsewhere to trade, to work or to seek safety.

Nowadays, the excellent universities and colleges also attract large numbers of students from all over the world, many of whom decide to stay and contribute to the vibrant diversity of the nation.

There is no compulsion to speak Welsh but many people deeply enjoy doing so. The lyrical nature of the language seems designed to produce pleasingly poetic sounds and opens the door to a treasure trove of culture. Even the smallest attempt at learning the basics will be much appreciated by the people you meet, even if they need to help you a little with some of the sounds.

The language is generally phonetic, so that each letter represents only one sound: what is written is what you say – but some of the sounds differ from English, as follows:

'a' as in 'apple'
'e' as in 'exit'
'i' as in 'ee'
'o' as in office
'u' sounds similar to the 'i' in 'win', but longer
'w' as in 'win' - serves as a vowel
'y' as the 'u' in 'cup', but longer – serves as a vowel
the famous 'll' is akin to the 'tl' sound in the English words 'antler' or 'Bentley'- but

you breathe out gently as you say it.
the Welsh 'ch' is similar to that in Johann Sebastian Bach, a highly regarded figure in Wales!
'dd' sounds like the 'th' in then
'th' sounds like the 'th' in thing

Websites
www.bwrdd-yr-iaith.org.uk (information on the Welsh language)
www.bbc.co.uk/wales/learnwelsh

A few helpful words and phrases

Good morning	Bore da
Good afternoon	Prynhawn da
Goodbye	Hwyl fawr
Good evening	Noswaith dda
Good health!/Cheers	Iechyd da!
Good night	Nos da
How are you?	Sut mae?
Very good	Da iawn
Welcome	Croeso
Welcome to Wales	Croeso i Gymru
fine thanks	iawn diolch
yes	ie
no	na
please	os gwelwch yn dda
Thank you	Diolch
Good	Da
small	bach
big	mawr
where is?	ble mae?
castle	castell
river	afon
food	bwyd
drink	diod
I'd like a pint of...	Hoffwn i beint o...
And a glass of...	a gwydriad o...
Where am I?	Ble ydw i?
I'm lost!	Dwi ar goll!
Where's the nearest cashpoint?	Ble mae'r twll yn y wal agosaf?

Graffeg books

Graffeg publish illustrated books about contemporary life in Wales.
Each book is focused on a particular interest: landscapes, food, lifestyle,
heritage, architecture, festivals, music, arts, sports and culture.
Graffeg books make wonderful guides, travelling companions and gifts.

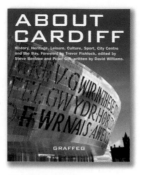

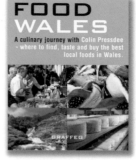

Landscape Wales
by David Williams,
foreword by Bryn Terfel.
- **Landscape Wales hardback
  £24.95**
- ISBN 0 9544334 1 6
- **Landscape Wales softback £12.95**
- ISBN 0 9544334 3 2 (English)
- **Tirlun Cymru softback £12.95**
- ISBN 0 9544334 5 9 (Welsh)

About Cardiff
by David Williams
foreword Trevor Fishlock.
- £12.95
- Publication October 2005
- Softback size 250 x 200mm
- 160 pages in full colour
- 117 colour illustrations
- ISBN 0 9544334 2 4

Food Wales
by Colin Pressdee.
- £12.95
- Publication October 2005
- Softback size 250 x 200mm
- 192 pages in full colour
- 157 colour illustrations
- ISBN 0 9544334 6 7

Welsh National Opera
Edited by Caroline Leech.
- £14.99
- Publication May 2006
- Softback size 250 x 200mm
- 192 pages in full colour
- Over 100 colour illustrations
- ISBN 1 905582 00 5

View our catalogue online www.graffeg.com

Visit our website for the
latest news and view the
Graffeg book list online
@ www.graffeg.com
Browse through books online
before you order. The new
'trade section' has news and
information about all our
books and includes details
about new titles.

**Book trade distributors
and wholesalers:**
Welsh Books Council.
Tel: 01970 624455
castellbrychan@cllc.org.uk
www.gwales.com

Gardners Books.
Tel: 01323 521777
custcare@gardners.com
www.gardners.com

Bertram Books.
Tel: 0870 429 6600
sales@bertrams.com
www.bertrams.com

Published by Graffeg.
Tel: 029 2037 7312
sales@graffeg.com
www.graffeg.com

GRAFFEG

Index A-F

Index G-N

Index 0-T

Index U-Y